Wisps of Wildfire

BY

F. W. BOREHAM, D.D.

Author of

The Drums of Dawn, A Witch's Brewing, When the Swans Fly High, The Blue Flame, The Three Half Moons, The Fiery Crags, A Temple of Topaz, The Nest of Spears, A Tuft of Comet's Hair, A Faggot of Torches, The Crystal Pointers, A Casket of Cameos, A Reel of Rainbow, Rubble and Roseleaves, Shadows on the Wall, A Bunch of Everlastings, Home of the Echoes, Whisper of God, The Other Side of the Hill, The Uttermost Star, The Silver Shadow, Faces in the Fire, Mushrooms on the Moor, The Golden Milestone, Mountains in the Mist, The Luggage of Life, &c, &c.

First published in 1924

Reprinted 2017

This book is unabridged and faithful to the original edition as published in 1924.

ISBN-10: 1-5217-5396-2
ISBN-13: 978-1-5217-5396-5

Publication arranged by Pioneer Library
Publisher of classic missions and devotional books

Printed by Kindle Direct Publishing

Also available for Kindle

For more information, visit pioneerflame.com

Table of Contents

PART I

PART II

PART III

BY WAY OF INTRODUCTION

Just as dusk was falling, I came, one summer evening, on a circular clearing in the bush, overgrown with heath and hyacinths, bracken and burrs. On a bare branch of a giant bluegum, a pair of jackasses were laughing to their hearts' content. Beside a fireplace that he had fashioned of a few rough stones, a bronzed and bearded swagman was sitting on a fallen tree-fern, enjoying his evening meal. We were soon talking of everything under the sun—the Dorsetshire village in which he was born; the feverish gold rush that lured him overseas; and the wayward gipsyings of later days. As we gossiped beside the dying embers, the sky became pyrotechnic with wildfire. It gleamed from every point of the compass. In the vivid radiance of each flash, every stick and stone around us stood out as clearly as at noon.

'Going far?' I inquired.

'I must make Wombat Creek tonight!'

'A dark trudge,' I observed; 'it'll take you all your time to keep the track!'

'Oh, yes,' he replied with a smile, as he rose picked up his billy, humped his swag and lit his pipe, 'but *a few wisps of wildfire will light things up a bit!*'

My Australian swagman is not the only pilgrim on the planet who has to follow a tortuous track in a poor light. It may be—who knows?—that a stray sentence somewhere in these pages will enable some uncertain wayfarer to discern more clearly the obscure path from which, in his confusion, he otherwise might have wandered.

FRANK W. BOREHAM.
Armadale, Melbourne, Australia
Easter, 1924.

PART I

I

MY WALKING-STICKS

A walking-stick is great company. That is why so many of us carry one. I know, of course, that other reasons for the habit are usually given. That is a way we mortals have. I very well remember a visit I paid one Monday to John Broadbanks at Silverstream. In those days John had an avenue of standard roses running all the way from the gate to the door of the Manse. After dinner we walked up and down this path admiring the autumn blooms. My attention was arrested by a beautiful blossom, snowy white; and, stooping to read the neat little tag, which had evidently been newly attached, I was surprised to greet the name of *Victor Hugo*.

'Dear me,' I exclaimed, 'I had always supposed that the *Victor Hugo* was a bright crimson!' John stepped forward in astonishment and examined, not only that particular label, but a dozen others in the immediate vicinity.

'Oh, that boy!' he groaned. 'I got him to come in for a few days to do odd jobs about the garden and the stable. I noticed that the labels on the roses were weather-beaten and illegible. I wrote out new ones,

9

and trusted him to tie them on. He must have got them all mixed up!'

Something very similar happens as we go through life. We attach reasons to our actions as we attach labels to our rose-trees. But some wicked sprite must have mixed them all up. For I never yet beheld, attached to any action, the reason that really prompted it. When, across the top of this sheet of paper, I wrote the words 'My Walking-Sticks,' and thus committed myself irrevocably to an essay on that enticing theme, it at once occurred to me that I ought to consult an encyclopaedia. The conventions of life seemed to demand it of me. An encyclopaedia is always worth its place on a man's shelves. It gives him the feeling that he has vast stores of knowledge available at a moment's notice. As a matter of fact, the encyclopaedia is a great illusion. The only kind of knowledge that a man finds of any real service in this world is the knowledge that he has acquired by hard toil and long experience. Still, there is something in *feeling* wealthy. My conscience told me that it was meet, right, and my bounden duty to consult an encyclopaedia. To show that I did my duty, and obeyed my conscience, not grudgingly, but cheerfully, I consulted two. I ought to have known better. It is always a mistake to consult two encyclopaedias. They invariably contradict each other; and it is never pleasant to get involved m a noisy brawl of that sort. It is better to consult one, and to accept its judgement as final. My conscience told me that it was my duty to consult an encyclopaedia. I spoiled my obedience by consulting *two*. We often overdo things.

The first encyclopaedia informed me, with that ponderous gravity which is the distinguishing feature of encyclopaedias, that a walking-stick is an insect—*cladomorphus phyllinus*—and belongs to the *phasmidae* of Brazil. I thanked the encyclopaedia as politely as possible, and returned it to the shelf none the poorer, I trust, for the wealth of wisdom it had imparted to me. I reached down the second. It deigned to mention that the term 'walking-stick' may denote a staff carried in the hand when walking. So far so good; I had myself suspected something of the kind. Indeed, I should have had no quarrel with this second encyclopaedia if it had stopped at that point. But it proceeded to give a reason for the custom; and, like John Broadbanks' hired boy, it tied on the wrong label, in the old days, it explained, every man carried a rapier or a sword. When the necessity no longer existed, men hesitated to go out empty-handed, a stick seemed a natural and harmless substitute. They therefore acquired the habit of carrying sticks.

Now the worst of tying name-tags to the rose-trees is that some captious and censorious person may come along and point out that the white rose is not, as its label alleges, a *Victor Hugo*. And the worst of giving reasons for such a practice as that which we are now considering is that somebody is sure to come along and declare that the reason given is the wrong one. In this case it is Mr. Clarence M. Lyman who challenges the verdict of the encyclopaedia. Mr. Lyman is an American, but he was delivering a lecture before the Society of British Architects when he so suddenly turned his attention to this matter of walking-sticks. Mr. Lyman will not hear of the sword theory. 'The fact is,' he says, 'that, when men acquired the habit of carrying umbrellas as a protection against threatening showers, they found themselves involved in constant loss. The day cleared up; they forgot that they had started out armed with umbrellas; and they left their property wherever they happened to be. To correct this costly habit, they got into the way of carrying sticks when the sky was clear and umbrellas when the day was cloudy. They thus schooled themselves to leave no place empty-handed.

I am sorry to have got entangled in this quarrel between the encyclopaedia and the American lecturer. But I can escape from the embarrassment by the simple process of appointing myself—as I have a perfect right to do—an arbitrator for the adjustment of their differences. And when I am called upon to decide between the *sword* theory of the encyclopaedia and the *umbrella* theory of the

American lecturer, I shall decide the matter in the most satisfactory way by summarily rejecting them both. A plague on both their houses! They are both wrong! They differ in detail; and with the pitiful little detail on which they differ no man who loves his walking-stick will have any patience at all. For they agree—to their shame be it said—in heaping insult and ignominy on all our walking-sticks. A walking-stick, so they both say, has no rights of its own, no merits of its own no justification for its own existence. It is purely and simply a stop-gap. In the one theory it takes the place of the rapier; in the other it takes the place of the umbrella; but in both it is merely a substitute. No man who has made a friend and confidant of his walking-stick will extend a moment's hospitality to either of these theories.

We carry walking-sticks for the reason that I stated in my opening sentence. A walking-stick is great company. Except in wet weather, when the necessities of the case demand an umbrella, I never go out without one. But let it be clearly understood that, on those occasions, the umbrella is a substitute for the walking-stick. The walking-stick is never a substitute for the umbrella. When I am compelled to take an umbrella, and to leave the stick, I feel as a man feels who leaves his dog yelping mournfully at the gate. I glance apologetically at the walking-stick as I pass up the hall and feel a little ashamed that I am preferring comfort to constancy. It is a proud and happy moment when, foul weather having passed, I can set off with my stick once more. A walking-stick is an excellent listener and an excellent talker—the two essentials of a perfect companionship. It never speaks when I am in the mood for silence. It never broaches uncongenial subjects. It never interrupts or contradicts. It never shows heat or irritation. It listens when I want it to listen: it is dumb when I want to be quiet: it becomes instantly garrulous in response to my wish.

The philosophers, looking at me over their spectacles, will tell me that my walking-stick never listens and never talks. Its speech, these wiseacres will tell me, is a kind of intellectual ventriloquism on my part. I throw my own voice into the stick and then attribute to it the things that I myself say. I assure these philosophers that, for once, they are mistaken. The voice of the stick is not my voice: it is the stick's voice. If it were my voice, any stick would suit any occasion. But that is not so. I have a number of sticks. Each has its own associations. Each has its own line of thought. One chatters to me of England; another rattles on about New Zealand; a third talks about Tasmania; and so on. Each brings to my mind its own set of people. It revives the memory of old familiar faces and old familiar places. In setting out for my walk, I seldom have any hesitation in deciding which stick to take. One or the other always seems to be the right one.

It matches my mood. I feel for it by a kind of instinct. It will bring to my mind things on which I am in the humour to dwell. It will talk on the subjects that I am most inclined to think about. It is just the companion for the day. The other sticks thoroughly understand: they cherish no resentment. For therein lies a further charm about my walking-sticks. They show no pique. They know no jealousy —of each other. They never take offence. I pick up one—the right one for the occasion—and set off down the street. The others must remain in the stand. But they submit with a good grace. It is only on wet days that they show displeasure. Between them and the umbrellas there is no fellowship at all. They feel that the umbrellas seize upon the bad weather as an occasion to supplant them.

The walking-stick and the umbrella have nothing, or next to nothing, in common. An umbrella is a complicated affair; the world was growing old before it was invented. The stick, on the contrary, is simplicity itself; it was the first thing that the first man handled. There are a few things—a very few—that came into the world in their final form. They are incapable of improvement. Of this small and select company, the walking-stick is a distinguished member. Save for a little polish and a little varnish, a little trimming and a little carving-all of them mere matters of adornment—there is no difference between the first walking-stick and the last. The walking-stick represents the great simplicities of life, and the simplicities are eternal. Our complicated and intricate mechanisms evolve themselves into existence and evolve themselves out again. They are the wonder of the world today and the laughing-stock of posterity tomorrow. In the lust for improvement they come, and in the lust for improvement they go. But there are things of which we never make a fuss. They are never the cynosure of wondering eyes. They just go on with their work generation after generation, century after century, age after age. There is no essential difference between the stick that I carry and the stick on which Mephibosheth limped. His would have served me just as well as my own; and mine would have been just as serviceable to him. The world's best things— and its best people—are of this modest and faithful order.

My walking-stick is an exquisitely simple contrivance. You can imagine nothing simpler: yet it is by means of it that I prove every day of my life that I am a man and not a brute. For the beasts that perish have no idea of supporting their frailty by means of adventitious aids. The sphinx, according to the ancient mythologies, was sharp enough to perceive this peculiarity of ours, and upon it he based his famous riddle. 'What animal,' the monster asked, 'walks in the morning upon *four* feet, at noon upon *two*, and in the evening upon *three*?' Everybody who answered the conundrum wrongly was instantly destroyed; and it was not until it occurred to Oedipus that man crawls upon all fours in infancy, strides erect in maturity, and hobbles on a stick in his old age, that the sphinx was silenced and Thebes delivered from its terror. My walking-stick is, therefore, a sceptre in disguise. Carrying it, I prove myself a king. It is the sign of my sublimity. It is the emblem and symbol of my manhood.

I like to think, too, that my walking-stick represents those inexpensive but invaluable things that never fail us when we need them most. Today I carry my stick for company. But there have been times when I have carried it because I could not move without it, and my blistered hands have shown how heavily I leaned upon it then. We are all of us liable to accident; I have had more than my share of them. We sustain injuries; we break our legs and sprain our ankles: we are reduced to sudden infirmity: and if we live long enough, we all grow old. Under such conditions, we need support: and the walking-stick becomes the benefactor of us all The millionaire, finding his frail limbs totter, buys for himself a stick; with all his wealth, he can obtain nothing better. And, among the poorest of the poor, there are none so indigent as to find a stick beyond their slender means. The old folk at the almshouses and benevolent institutions all have their sticks. The walking-stick brings plutocrat and peasant to a common level. My walking-stick stands for all those essential and dependable things that, amidst the emergencies and calamities of life, seem to be waiting for our call.

These things, I say, never fail us when we need them most. I often think of that as I recall some of my experiences at Mosgiel. I noticed that, when those Scottish settlers were dying, there was one passage of Scripture on which they invariably insisted. They always asked for the twenty-third Psalm. I think they preferred the paraphrased version.

> The Lord's my Shepherd, I'll not want:
>   He makes me down to lie
> In pastures green; He leadeth me
>   The quiet waters by.

The third verse was always particularly impressive on those occasions:

> Yea, though I walk in death's dark vale,
>   Yet I will fear none ill;
> For Thou art with me: and Thy rod
>   And staff me comfort still.

'Aye,' said old Hughie Cargill, as I read the verses to him a few hours before he passed from us, 'I've aye noticed that ye maist need a staff when ye're ganging doonhill!'

He was entering the valley, and, like Daniel Webster, he found the rod and the staff a great comfort.

'Read those words again!' said the great American statesman on the last day of his life. The friend at the bedside repeated the Psalm When he reached the fourth verse Mr. Webster raised his hand.

'Ah, that's it,' he murmured feebly, '*the rod and the staff!*' It is *the rod and the staff* that comfort a man at the last!

II

SCARLET AND GOLD

There broke upon me this morning an apocalyptic vision—a vision of *scarlet and gold!*

The *scarlet* was just a pillar-box, resplendent in all the bravery of a new coat of paint and varnish.

The *gold* was a canary, trembling with the wild excitement of his escape from his accustomed cage!

The *scarlet* was crowned by the gold! The canary, that is to say, was perched upon the pillar-box. In *Mountains in the Mist* I have told the story of the 'Canary at the Pole.' I must supplement it today by placing on record the story of the 'Canary on the Pillar-box.'

Sitting on the front of a cable-car, I was on my way into the city. It was a delightful morning, and everything about me was at its best. All at once, I was startled by a splash of gold, almost within reach of my hand. It was a bird, flying low, and evidently unused to flying at all. It almost struck the front of the tram-car; and, on reaching the pillar-box on the edge of the pavement, seemed glad to alight upon it.

'Poor little beggar!' exclaimed the driver of the car compassionately. 'There'll be very little left of him by nightfall!'

'Very little left of him by nightfall!' All that was left of him by nightfall was a little heap of ruffled gold, lifeless and cold, lying under the elm. Or, perhaps, less even than *that* was left of him. For, now that I come to think of it, I distinctly remember seeing a big black cat, with a wicked look in his eye, sunning himself on a wall near by.

Nightfall! But what a day it was that closed with that sad and tragic nightfall! Think of it!

Dawn! He sings in his cage at the window; sings, not *of* the cage, but *in* it. He sings the song that exiles ever sing: the song of home! He sings of the glowing sunshine of those tropic isles to which his happy tribe belongs; he sings of waving palm-trees and terraced vineyards; he sings of a soft luxurious clime to which stern winter never comes. And, singing, he forgets the cage and the window and the bustling street outside. He is singing the song of liberty, the song of independence, the song of home!

Day! The morning brings the chance of freedom. His young mistress feeds him, gives him sugar and seed and water, and—leaves the door insecurely fastened! He flies lightly against it. and it swings upon its hinges! He perches on the wire at the open doorway and faces the issues—the cage behind; the great, great world beyond! He is a prisoner; a pampered prisoner, it is true; but a prisoner none the less. Shall he go back to a life of ease and luxury —and prison bars? Or shall he go out to a life of struggle and hardship—and liberty? He makes the decision that any really gallant spirit would have made. And, two minutes later, the empty cage hangs in the window to tell the young mistress the silent story of her sad bereavement. The canary is out in the wide, wide world. He has his liberty; but his liberty soon becomes a burden to him. He grows dazed and confused. He tries to fly across the street; but to his unpractised wings, it is a long, long way. In his desperation he thinks to settle on the moving tram, but, as it draws near, it seems like a huge monster cruelly pursuing him. By a frantic effort he struggles to the pillar-box. And the rest of his sad story is already known to us.

Now this is tragic enough, but it represents a greater tragedy still. At least, it represents two; Perhaps even three. In his *Little Journey to the Home of Thomas Huxley*, Elbert Hubbard says that 'two tragedies confront man on his journey through life —one when he wants a thing and cannot get it; the other when he gets a thing and then discovers that he does not want it.' Huxley wanted a surgeon's diploma—till he got it! And, when he got it, he suddenly realized that a surgeon's life had no attraction for him. Now both of these tragedies are symbolized by my vision of scarlet and gold.

Here is the canary in his cage at the window, longing for freedom—the tragedy of wanting a thing and not getting it!

Here is the canary in possession of his freedom, yet failing to enjoy it—the tragedy of having a thing and finding you do not want it!

And, hard upon the heels of these two tragedies, comes the third and culminating tragedy—the dead canary under the elm at sunset!

I wish—no harm in wishing, however ridiculous the wish—I wish that, as our little canary paused, undecided, for just a moment at the doorway of his cage, I could have had a little talk with him. I wish I could have pointed out to him the fact that one of the most impressive lessons that history has taught to men is the fact that every blessing is a curse to the man who is unready for it. Wealth is a good thing; yet many a man, unprepared for its enjoyment and administration, and totally ignorant of its responsibilities and obligations, has been destroyed by sudden affluence. Power is a good thing; but power in the hands of a man—or a mob—unfitted for power leads to inevitable tyranny and disaster. All the most sacred and most delicate relationships of life are good things—the relationship between man and maid; the relationship between husband and wife; the relationship between parent and child;

and so on—yet, from the abuse of these relationships, on the part of those who have shown themselves unprepared for them, the most revolting infelicities of life, arise.

In precisely the same way, freedom is a most excellent thing. The men who have lived and died for freedom are the heroes of the ages. Yet, if experience has demonstrated one thing more clearly than another, it is that freedom is only a good thing when the man—or the bird—is ready for freedom. When the American slaves were suddenly set free, their emancipation threatened to become an unspeakable fiasco, an irretrievable disaster. They were free, but they were not ready for freedom. Happily, men like Booker Washington, himself a slave, saw the danger and devoted their lives to the task of averting it. In his *Up from Slavery*, Booker Washington describes the crisis. He recalls the historic edict. 'There was no sleep that night,' he says; 'all was excitement and expectancy. Early in the morning we were all sent for. The proclamation was read: we were told that we were free and could go when and where we pleased. My mother, who was standing by my side, leaned over and kissed her children, while tears of joy ran down her cheeks. There was great rejoicing, followed by wild scenes of ecstasy.' What is this but our little canary escaping from its cage at last? But let us read on: 'The wild rejoicing did not last long,' Booker

Washington says. 'By the time the coloured people returned to their cabins, there was a marked change in their feelings. The great responsibility of being free seemed to take possession of them. It was very much like suddenly turning a youth of ten or twelve years out into the world to provide for himself. Within a few hours the wild rejoicing ceased and a feeling of deep gloom seemed to pervade the slave quarters. Now that they were in actual possession of freedom, they found freedom a much more serious business than they had ever for one moment expected.' What is this but our little canary, bewildered by the traffic of the busy street, wishing himself back in his cage at the window? Had it not been for the magnificent work of Mr. Booker Washington, and the schools and colleges which he established for the training of the coloured people, the emancipation of the slaves might have taken its place as the greatest catastrophe of American history. Mr. Booker Washington devoted all his energies to the task of saving his people from the fate of my little canary.

Or take the French Revolution. After ages of tyranny, the people were free at last! The tocsin had sounded, and they had risen in their might. But the hideous orgies and frightful excesses of the Revolution stand for all time as a gruesome and ghastly monument to the fact that it is easier to make a nation free than to make it fit for freedom.

The unfitness of the French people for their newfound freedom cost France her best blood and her best brains; and she has never recovered from the stupendous impoverishment that she then sustained.

I wish I could have warned my little canary that life plays strange pranks with us. It takes constant watching. It maliciously ordains, for instance, that each style of life shall create and foster an appetite for a different style; yet, at the same time, it deliberately unfits us for the career with which it tantalizes us. The man who spends a sedentary life in classroom or office or study feels an increasing desire for a life of activity and adventure. He thinks that it would be glorious to burst the bands of habit and go big-game hunting in Africa, or exploring in South America, or searching for the secrets embedded in the ice and snow of polar realms. Yet whilst his tranquil life creates and inflames this lust of excitement, it simultaneously unfits him for the very enterprises of which he dreams so wistfully. Every day his sinews get softer: every day his blood gets slower: every day renders him less capable of such tough tasks. In contrast with this, the adventurer dreams fondly of a life of restfulness and seclusion. Every evening, beside his camp fire, he promises himself that, one great day, he will say good-bye to prairies and forests and jungles, and will seek a home beside some village green. But every day fastens more firmly upon him the love of danger and the passion of the unexplored. He dreams more and more fondly of the rural cottage with the lattice windows: yet his restless and roving spirit becomes every day less and less capable of entering into its felicity.

Charles Darwin has told us of the pang with which this strange law was brought home to him. He had always promised himself that, when the tension of life relaxed a little, he would abandon himself to the pleasures of art, music, and literature. 'Up to the age of thirty,' he says, 'poetry of many kinds, such as the works of Milton, Gray, Byron, Wordsworth, Coleridge, and Shelley, gave me great pleasure. Even as a boy I took intense delight in Shakespeare. Pictures, too, gave me considerable, and music very great delight.' During the years of his active career he had, perforce, to neglect these enjoyments, but he often said that, as soon as circumstances permitted, he would, with the greatest eagerness, return to them. The time came when circumstances did permit; but, alas, his taste had withered with the years! 'To my unspeakable sorrow,' he sadly says, 'I cannot endure to read a line of poetry. I have tried lately to enjoy Shakespeare, but I found it so intolerably dull that it nauseated me. I have even lost my taste for pictures and music. I retain some fondness for beautiful scenery, but it does not cause me the exquisite delight which it formerly did. My mind seems to have become a mere machine for grinding general laws out of large collections of facts.' Such is the tyranny of the cage! The cage makes the fields and the woods appear unutterably enticing, yet, all the time, it is robbing the poor bird of the very capacities that would make liberty delightful!

There is yet another consideration to which my little canary should have given due weight before embarking on his tragic enterprise. If, before spreading his wings, he had consulted me, I should have pointed out to him that he is only a unit, an individual, a solitary; and, as such, he is bound to go to the wall. There are only two kinds of creatures in the world—the wolves and the sheep. There are, that is to say, the fierce things and the gentle things. At first blush it would seem as if the gentle things must swiftly be exterminated. Tennyson says in "In Memoriam" that Nature is 'red in tooth and claw.' And, again, in "Maud", he says:

> For Nature is one with rapine,
>   A harm no preacher can heal;
> The mayfly is torn by the swallow,
>   The sparrow spear'd by the shrike,
> And the whole little wood where I sit
>   Is a world of plunder and prey!

With Tennyson, the lamb is always in the fangs of the wolf; the meek-eyed antelope is slain by the pitiless panther; the dove is done to death by the

29

hawk. But if this is the truth, and the whole truth, how is it that in the age-long struggle for existence the gentler creatures are getting all the best of it? The contest between the gazelle and the hyena seems a most unequal one; yet the fact is that, whilst the gazelle is constantly multiplying, zoologists are seriously concerned about the future of the hyena. 'The sparrow is spear'd by the shrike,' says Tennyson; yet, in spite of that uncomfortable circumstance, the sparrow is doing marvellously well, whilst shrikes are very seldom seen.

Prince Kropotkin once wrote a most fascinating book to show that, on all the steppes and plains and prairies of the world, the harmless creatures are multiplying amazingly, whilst the beasts of prey are dying out. And why? Simply because the gentler things understand the secret of cooperation. The sparrow, seeing the feast, flies off and spreads the news among its fellows. Lapwings, gathering together and attacking in massed formation, can drive off an eagle. Similarly, wagtails will overwhelm a sparrow-hawk, and swallows a falcon. Wild horses and zebras, threatened by a beast of prey, rush together and, standing with their faces to the foe, are impregnable. Prince Kropotkin has pages and pages of such illustrations. The gentle creatures of the wild are more than holding their own, and they are doing it by means of their community instinct, their genius for cooperation. But what allies has our little canary in the world into which he soars? He goes out a unit—friendless, mateless, helpless—and, therefore, he goes out to die.

That is the worst of seclusion, whether in a cage or in a cloister. The sheltered soul gets out of touch with life. The shelter may be very attractive, just as a cage may be made very beautiful. But the peril is none the less grave on that account. 'Mid pleasures and palaces there's no place like home; yet, even home threatens our boys and girls with destruction if it protects without preparing them. The monastic system is at least logical. It recognizes that the sheltered souls in the cloisters are unfitted by their very seclusion for the fierce combat of the busy world; and it takes good care that they are never exposed to it. They pass from their cloisters to their graves. But with these dear homes of ours it is quite otherwise. These laughing little madcaps of ours will not long remain under the kindly and beneficent restraints of home. The time soon comes for them to go out into the rough and tumble of life. They will have to mix with all sorts and conditions of men—good, bad, and indifferent. They will come into touch with life on its sinister and seamy side; they will see things and hear things that their parents would gladly have given their lives to spare them. Yet no reasonable person would wish it otherwise. The finest strains of character are only evolved under such conditions. The sensible parent will shed no tears about it; he will sternly resolve that home, for his children, shall not only be a shelter but a training-ground. He will reflect on the pathos of the dead canary under the elm-tree, and will register a vow that none of the young people in his home shall, through any fault of his, become the victims of an even more desolating tragedy.

The canary—having its liberty, yet unable to enjoy it—has, therefore, some vitally important things to say. Many a man, for example, looks forward to enjoying, in his later years, a freedom that, in his busier days, has been impossible to him. If he pays heed to the canary, he will be at some pains to fit himself for the freedom that he so pleasurably anticipates. It would be a thousand pities if, in his case, as in the case of the canary, freedom proved only a disappointment after all. 'If,' said Darwin ruefully, 'if I had to live my life over again, I would make it a rule to read a little poetry and hear a little music every week; for perhaps the parts of my brain now atrophied would thus have been kept active through use.' A man should, during his strenuous years, keep his soul in tune with the things that he hopes to enjoy when the strain is relaxed.

And, as I pursue this line of thought, the canary on the pillar-box suddenly assumes a still more serious tone. He reminds me that, one day, I shall find my cage door open and shall plume my wings for flight. One day I shall leave the window and fly out into the infinite. It would be the tragedy of tragedies if, when that day comes, my great adventure fills me with nothing but bewilderment and alarm. Within the narrow limits of my present life, I must seek so to develop all my faculties and powers that, when the door opens, I may enter into my freedom with confidence and greet the unknown with a song.

III

BREAKING THE NEWS

As a general rule, things that are broken are broken by the clumsy. When eggs are broken, or when dishes are broken, or when promises are broken, it is because some one has blundered. But to this general rule there is one striking exception. Careless people may break our china; careless people may break our hearts; but, when it comes to breaking the news, careless people would be worse than useless. However dexterous and skilful at ordinary tasks, the man who is called upon to break the news feels himself to be destitute of all the courtesies and delicacies of human life.

One of the most distinguished of our Australian artists, Mr. John Longstaff, has a particularly fine picture bearing the title of this chapter. It is the painting that won for him his travelling scholarship. It represents the interior of a cottage, the door of which stands open. A stalwart and bearded miner, grey and kindly, is doing his best to convey to the young mother, who holds a baby in her arms, the cruel tidings that a terrible catastrophe has overtaken the mine, and that her husband is numbered among the victims. When the news-breaker entered, the woman was evidently preparing the evening meal. The plates are warming by the fire; the table is laid; a fork on the floor has fallen from her hand in her sudden agitation. Through the open doorway the bearers can be seen bringing the body to the stricken home. Nobody can look carefully into the picture without recognizing that, in the person of this rugged but fatherly miner, who is so eager to mitigate the grief of the bereaved woman, Mr. Longstaff has given us the news-breaker at his best.

If, at such a task, any man can succeed, this man should be able to do so. Into the noble lines of his fine face the artist has crowded a representation of all those rare and subtle qualities that a person so situated imperatively requires. For the man who would essay so delicate an undertaking must possess a spirit so extremely sensitive and so intensely sympathetic that he can feel every emotional tremor and vibration that his looks and words excite; his eye must be so quick and so familiar with all the lights and shadows that play across the human face that he will instantly recognize and accurately interpret every signal of distress that appears on his poor companion's countenance; he must have a mind so serenely calm and so perfectly disciplined that he is always superior to, and in command of, the trying situation that so swiftly develops; and he must have a touch so gentle and yet so strong that the mere pressure of his hand inspires tranquillity and courage.

In every other art—music, painting, oratory—somebody has at some time risen to super-excellence, but in the art of breaking the news nobody has ever left the plane of mediocrity. The man who could do it well has not yet been born. Among all the excellent of the earth—past and present—I can think of only One who would have adorned so difficult a situation; and, unfortunately, there is no record of His having actually done it. On more than one occasion He broke good news to those to whom His words seemed incredible. In the home at Bethany and in the house of Jairus He told the mourners that their dead should live; but there is no instance of His doing such work as the miner is doing in the picture. It is easy to imagine His doing it; perhaps that is why there is no record; inspiration does not waste words in describing scenes that we can readily construct for ourselves.

Moreover, there is another reason. No mere written record could have conveyed to our minds the *spirit* of the sad occasion. It could have told us the words that were spoken; but words have cruel limitations. You cannot in words describe a perfume. In breaking the news, so much depends upon the accents in which the words are spoken, the looks by which they are accompanied, and the touch by which they are attended, that a written description of such an episode must of necessity have been strangely cold and unconvincing. But the lack is no real loss. I can see the incomparable grace with which He would have discharged the painful task. With a composure that would have radiated bravery, and a tenderness that would have fallen on a bruised spirit like a healing benediction, He would have spoken the soft but desolating words. But He is the only One who could have done it. In this respect, as in every other, He stands peerless and alone.

Words are clumsy tools to work with. A man trying to break the news with words is like a jeweller trying to mend a gold watch with a pickaxe. But there is this essential difference between the two men; the jeweller is not shut up to the pickaxe; he has alternatives; there lie on his table a variety of delicate instruments perfectly suited to his task. But the man who is required to break the news has no alternative implements. He must work with words—or nothing; and I once made the discovery that the task may be most successfully performed with *nothing*. It was the only occasion on which I was able to satisfy myself that I had, in the true sense of the word, broken the news. But I will come to that presently.

If I understand the phrase, it means to impart the news little by little in order to soften the blow. I have often attempted to do this by means of words, and have failed every time. I have compared notes with others, and have not yet met a man who, working with words, had met with better success. In my experience, and in the experience of those with whom I have conferred, the force of a blow is seldom or never softened by the mere jugglery of phrases. However skilfully you order your behaviour and select your words, there comes a second at which the person to whom you are speaking has no suspicion of the communication that you are about to make, and, right on its heels, there comes a second in which, like a flash of lightning, there darts into your poor companion's mind the full and vivid realization of the truth. The stage at which the revelation is unsuspected, and the stage at which it is realized, are separated from each other by a space of time so brief as to be microscopically infinitesimal. As I look at Mr. Longstaff's picture I can see that the sturdy and sympathetic character of the good-natured miner is a tower of strength to the woman in her sorrow; but it is clear that only the smallest fraction of time intervened between the moment at which she suspected nothing and the moment at which she knew all. So true is it that you cannot mend a watch with a pickaxe; you cannot break the news with words.

Written words are just as bad. Hobart, my old Tasmanian home, is a holiday resort; people from all over Australia go there for the delightful scenery and the bracing mountain air. Whilst I was there, there came to the city a Mrs. Hargreaves, the wife of a Sydney solicitor. She had sustained a severe nervous breakdown, and had been ordered a long rest in Tasmania. Her husband was unable to accompany her. She was staying at a boarding-house near to the church. She often attended the services, and I got to know her pretty well. One afternoon I received a telephone message from the proprietor of the boarding-house, who happened to be a member of the church, telling me that Mrs. Hargreaves was in great trouble. I hurried round at once. I found her distracted with grief. When she was able to command some measure of self-possession, she pointed to a telegram on the mantelpiece. I took it down and read: '*Am very ill; please come at once.—Tom.*' I tried to comfort her by remarking that, fortunately, the *Oonah* was sailing for Sydney next day, and I added that, in all probability, her husband would be better before she could reach him. My words only threw her into another paroxysm of weeping.

'No, no, no!' she cried, wringing her hands. 'Tom's dead! He was dead before the telegram was sent.'

I told her that she had no right to jump to such a melancholy conclusion; but she would not hear me.

'He's dead!' she repeated. 'He would never have said "*Please come at once*"; he would have known that, as soon as I learned of his illness, I should hurry to his side. He's dead, dead, *dead!*' And he was.

The fact is that love lends a quickened perception to the faculties. Love knows; love remembers; love understands. The would-be news-breaker who sent the telegram prided himself on a particularly clever and considerate artifice; but love saw through it at a glance. The words that seemed to convey only a part of the truth told the whole of it. It is almost impossible by means of words—spoken or written— to administer the knowledge gradually; the tools are too clumsy.

But I have not yet told of the case on which I came nearer to success than on any other similar occasion. It was the one instance in which I was able, very largely, to dispense with words. We were just rising from tea one beautiful evening in the early summer when the telegraph boy rode up on his bicycle. I tore open the envelope and read: '*Please tell Mr. and Mrs. Millington that Stanley has been killed in action in France.*' Mr. and Mrs. Millington are among the nicest people I know; Stanley was their only boy. He was one of the most promising scholars and one of the finest athletes of his generation. His parents and his three young sisters were justly proud of him. I thought of the home—the walls covered with his portraits, the rooms adorned by the trophies he had won. Why should I be called upon to extinguish all its light and shatter all its happiness?

With a heavy heart I set out on my cruel mission, wondering at every step how I could temper to my poor friends the severity of the blow. When I came to the house—a pretty suburban home—I heard, issuing from within, the sounds of boisterous mirth. The girls were evidently having a romp before bedtime. My heart failed me; and I took a turn or two up and down the street before approaching the gate. Then I pulled myself together and braced myself for the ordeal. I rang the bell, and even its music seemed incongruous. Mrs. Millington herself came to the door. She was full of smiles and cordial welcome. 'Was Mr. Millington in?' Mr. Millington was not in; but he would not be long; I was urged to come in and wait. I was inclined to go away and to return later; but I feared that such behaviour might appear strange and lead to premature suspicion. Mrs. Millington took me into the drawing-room; we talked a little—a very little—about the weather and the health of our respective families; and then we lapsed into silence. A vague feeling crept over me that perhaps silence would do my sad work more gently and more gradually than speech. Except for an occasional word of a severely commonplace kind, nothing was said for some minutes. I knew that Mrs. Millington would slowly come to feel that this silence was not quite natural; I knew that it would very soon occur to her that I had not made my usual inquiries concerning Stanley; and I knew that when, in the silence, the first faint suspicion crossed her mind, she would reflect for a moment before she spoke.

Things happened exactly as I had foreseen. In the fading light of the summer evening, I watched the shadow creeping over her face—the reflection of the deeper shadow creeping over her heart. I saw her anxiety growing more acute as her suspicion deepened. Then, rising and coming towards me, she said quietly: 'You have come to bring us bad news?' There was no need for reply. I took her hand and led her back to her chair. She buried her face in her hands and the merciful relief of tears was richly ministered to her. It was the only case that I ever witnessed in which the news was really *broken*. It came to her little by little, and she was able to summon all the resources of her womanhood to meet it. I could not help contrasting her case with that of her husband and her daughters. In the nature of things, I had to break the news to them by means of words; it was crudely and clumsily done; the strong man cried aloud in his anguish, and the grief of the sisters was a piteous thing to see.

Now why does silence break the news so much more skilfully than speech? The answer is obvious. Silence is the eloquence of Nature; and, in the art of breaking the news, Nature is incomparable. She has the most bewildering astonishments to impart; yet she contrives to communicate them so gradually and so slowly that, so far from shocking us, she scarcely awakens our sense of wonder. If the knowledge that we now possess of the universe had been suddenly communicated to the philosophers of Egypt, Assyria, or Greece, they would have been dumbfounded. We, on the other hand, scarcely think it worth reading about or talking about; we yawn in unutterable boredom if an enthusiast on the subject becomes too garrulous. In the art of breaking the news—the art of imparting sensational information so gradually that the announcement is robbed of

all excitement and surprise—Nature is an expert. Nor are her achievements in this regard limited to matters of universal magnitude and world-wide import. She deals with the individual as considerately and as skilfully as she deals with the race. Many of the experiences of life, viewed remotely and hypothetically, appear intolerable; we imagine that, under certain circumstances, life would not be worth living; but when, in the course of Nature, the imaginary becomes the actual, we are astonished at the fortitude with which we bear it. Nature breaks the news to us very gently; she lays the burden, little by little upon o shoulders; and the thing that once we dreaded as insupportable, we eventually endure with a smile.

Very often, in visiting the sick, I have been warned on no account to give the patient the impression that he is about to die; and I have invariably respected the wisdom that suggested the admonition. In certain cases, the horror of death might precipitate death; the patient should be encouraged to fight for life as long as there is the shadow of a hope. But I have known other cases— hopeless cases—in which I was asked to break to the patient the news that recovery was impossible. The relatives felt that the sufferer was entitled to the solemn knowledge, yet dreaded the effect of the fateful communication. But their fears were baseless. Whilst I have never known a person of healthy body and healthy mind who did not recoil from the thought of death, I have, on the other hand, never known a dying person to be seriously perturbed by such an intimation. Nature has her own wonderful way of breaking the news; she does it in the silence and does it very cleverly; there may be a tear or two, but that is all.

With similar considerateness she deals with those who grow old. The inevitable penalty of old age is the constant losses of earlier companions. But, m her solicitude and courtesy, Nature meets this contingency—which would otherwise have been extremely painful—by deadening the sensibilities of age to the consciousness of poignant bereavement. Dr. Oliver Wendell Holmes speaks of a mysterious 'black drop' which, in old age, is mercifully infused into body and soul. In a poem entitled "The Blunted Edge," a modern minstrel describes the working of this mystic potion. An old man sips his broth and reads his paper beside the fire. His daughters whisper at a window. They have received a letter saying that the old man's favourite sister has died, and they dread to tell him; the shock, they fancy, may hasten his own end. But another thought occurs to them. The sister reflects:

> Ah, you remember how he loved our mother!
> And yet, last summer, after she had died,
> He never seemed to take it hard at all.
> He seemed too much resigned, too much himself.
> It would have killed him twenty years ago!

That is the point: 'It would have killed him twenty years ago,' whereas, now, he takes it calmly. A few minutes later the old man reads in his newspaper of his sister's death; and he accepts it with similar submission.

> . . . So Adelaide is dead!
> Well, she was restless—go and go she must.
> First to this place, then that place, till at last
> She settled in Nevada. As for me
> Here I am still, and I shall count my hundred.
> Well, well, well, well, so Adelaide is dead!

In extreme old age the loss that would once have seemed like the shipwreck of all life's fortunes falls as the fluttering to the ground of a faded roseleaf.

During Tennyson's last illness, his doctor told him of a villager near by who, dying at the age of ninety, pined to see his bed-ridden wife lying in the next room. She was carried in; he stretched out his shrunken hand, pressed hers, and said in a husky voice 'Come soon!' That was all. The separation, which would once have been crushing in its severity, was over. Nature mercifully attunes us to the march of events; she reconciles us to the inevitable; she breaks the news with incomparable kindliness and skill.

The black drop does its work. We become insensible to things that, at one time, would have broken our hearts. That is why a man should make instant response to every sweet and sacred impression that comes to him from this world or from the world unseen. For the time will come when his tenderest emotions will be blunted, and the beautiful things that once fascinated him, but which he then spurned, will appeal to his responseless soul in vain.

IV

A TANGLED SKEIN

I

My fingers have often itched to set down the story of Mary Creighton, just as she told it to me that day under the apple-tree, but, until now, my pen has been chained. A newspaper that came last week, however, contains announcements which have effectually brushed away the scruples that I cherished.

Mary Creighton was not her real name: her real name was much prettier, or she made it seem so to me. None of the names that I shall mention are real names. Mary herself was, for years, an inscrutable mystery to me. She was to everybody. Indeed, until that lovely afternoon she made her great confession, I never understood her and I never met anybody who did. A very general feeling prevailed in Mosgiel that, away back in the unforgotten years of Mary's life, a tragedy was buried somewhere; but nobody knew its nature. Innumerable guesses were made: but they were all contradictory, and, therefore, unsatisfactory. No theory squared with all the facts.

And so it came to pass that the little township gave it up. Mary came to be regarded as a riddle that everybody had asked, but of which nobody knew the answer.

Mary lived by herself in a cottage on the hillside. From her door, which invariably stood open, she commanded a fine view of the entire plain and its encircling hills.

'You should be here in the early morning,' she said to me one afternoon, as we stood together outside the door, admiring this extensive prospect. 'It's a wonderful sight. Old Blanche Bradshaw, who lives just round the ridge, often tells me that when she saw it first, fifty years ago, the Plain was a lake, and there was deep water where the farms now stand. And the ghost of the old lake comes back every night. When I open my door of a morning, I can see neither trees nor homesteads. The white mist lies all along the Plain, just like a sheet of water, and it looks for all the world as if Blanche's old lake had come back again.'

Mary was not a member of the church. She would not hear of it. Whenever I broached the matter she immediately changed the subject and left me mystified. The guessers were agreed in saying that Mary and her husband were living separately; I quickly came to the conclusion that they were right; yet why they should be separated I could not for the life of me imagine. As far as I could see, they were as fond of each other as a pair of lovers.

'You'll often be going to town?' she asked one day, soon after my settlement at Mosgiel; and I told her that I usually spent Mondays in Dunedin.

'Well,' she went on, 'would it be out of your way to drop in, every now and again, at a house in Queen Street and ask for Robert Creighton? You needn't stay; but just pass the time of day, and see how he looks, and be sure and let me know if you think he wants anything.'

Mary often called in at the Manse, generally on a Tuesday. She never asked if I had seen Robert the day before; but I could see that she was on tenterhooks until, being alone together, I broached the subject. Sometimes she would bring a little parcel—warm socks or a muffler or a pair of knitted gloves—for me to take next time I went; and occasionally she would call early on Monday morning with a little packet of cakes or scones or a jelly. There was never a specific message, however; I was never entrusted with a note or a letter; I was never requested to ask him anything.

When first I called on Robert he was extremely uncommunicative. I told him that a lady at Mosgiel had asked me to call on him. He smiled—sadly, I thought—told me that he was well, and gave me to understand by his manner that there was no more to be said. The room in which he lived was small but cosy; and I noticed a portrait of Mary—taken, perhaps, twenty years earlier—hanging on the wall. After a while his tongue loosened a little. When he was convinced of my trustworthiness, he began to ask after Mary. Was she well? Did I think that she was quite equal to all the work of the cottage? And once, after some years, he asked with a moistening of the eyes, Was she ageing? He, too, occasionally entrusted me with parcels—generally books and papers—but in his case, as in hers, there was never a note, a letter, a message or a direct inquiry. This went on for years. I watched them growing gradually older, growing perceptibly feebler, and growing all the while in tender solicitude for each other.

II

Robert was the first to go. He died very suddenly. I had called, as usual, on the Monday. He seemed well, and asked more questions than usual, particularly in regard to Mary's appearance. Was she as upright as ever? Did she look careworn or unhappy? Was her hair very white? Did it seem a struggle for her to climb the hill to the cottage? He started to ask another. I fancied that he wished to inquire whether Mary seemed lonely; but his voice caught and he turned it off into some meaningless remark about the weather. As I left, he slipped a sovereign into my hand and begged me to get any little thing that would comfort or brighten her. On the Thursday I received a telegram from his landlady. I caught the next train, but he was dead before I could reach him. He left a will bequeathing everything to Mary; and he told his landlady to ask me to bury him.

Poor Mary was disconsolate. I never saw grief quite like hers. To begin with, it was so exclusively hers. Nobody else knew of it; nobody could offer sympathy; nobody suspected that the gentle little lady on the hillside was overwhelmed in anguish so terrible. And, to make things worse, she was so helpless. She could do nothing. There is a melancholy consolation in being permitted to perform or superintend the last sad offices that we render to the dead; but even this poor comfort was denied to her. She could only sit in her cottage and weep apart. Others were doing—and doing without emotion—what it should have been her sad privilege to do. It was after the first storm of her grief had spent itself, after the first bitterness had passed, that she suddenly found it in her heart to unburden herself. The outburst of confidence was quite spontaneous; I had no idea that she was about to tell me her story, and I fancied that she herself was surprised at finding herself breaking the silence of the years. It was a beautiful afternoon in the late spring-time; the apple-trees in front of the cottage were a mass of blossom; and, on a seat that stood between two of the finest of them, we sat talking.

'It all happened in the early days,' she said. 'We were young and silly and wicked; and we did dreadful things without knowing how dreadful they were. Robert and I came out from the Old Country with our parents in the days of the gold rush in Australia. Everybody was talking about the diggings. Robert's father and my father were both having hard times; and they decided to try their luck. Robert and I had known each other as children; we had attended the same school; everybody regarded us as sweethearts. On the ship we were thrown a good deal together; and although we were never formally engaged, it was understood that we were to marry as soon as the exigencies of our new life rendered such a settlement possible.

'All went well until we reached Australia. Then we had to part. Robert's mother, my mother and I stayed in Sydney, whilst our fathers and Robert went on to the diggings. Then the trouble began. Robert was young and eager, and he caught the gold fever in its worst form. He seldom came to Sydney to see me and, even when he did, he seemed to be thinking far more of his gold than of me. I was very lonely. I used to count the days to his coming, and perhaps I did not make sufficient allowance for the excitement of his new life. In Sydney I got to know Philip Bryce. He was open-hearted and full of fun;

he was unselfish and courteous; and to me he was exceedingly attentive and kind. But it was purely a casual friendship until I took it into my head that Robert had grown tired of me. Then, perhaps, I gave Philip more encouragement than I should have done. I fancy that I had some vague notion of winning Robert back to me by making him jealous of Philip. At any rate, when Robert came again, talking nothing but gold, gold, gold, I talked nothing but Philip, Philip, Philip. But my wickedness met with its just reward. My stupid words had a diametrically opposite effect to that for which I had hoped. Robert lost all patience with me. He rose in anger; told me that I could have Philip if I wanted him; and, to my horror, went off mumbling something about Maggie.

'Maggie! Who was Maggie? Maggie, I learned later, was the daughter of John Marchant, who kept the Diggers' Rest.

The Diggers' Rest was not, in the ordinary sense, an hotel; it was a store, a shelter, and a place in which diggers of the better class might spend an evening, reading, writing, or at games. John Marchant looked after the business side of the place and took charge of any gold that successful diggers cared to entrust to his custody, whilst Mrs. Marchant and Maggie attended to the housework. Maggie was a pretty girl, tall, ripe-figured, of bright complexion and auburn hair. I did not sleep that night. It had never occurred to me that my silly prattle about Philip might have this effect. Robert told me afterwards that he had never given a serious thought to Maggie until that night. When I arose next morning, Robert was gone. Three months later I heard that he and Maggie were married. I was proud; I felt that I had been spurned, insulted, degraded; I determined that he should see how little I cared. Within four months of Robert's marriage to Maggie, I was married to Philip!'

III

'It was a miserable business. Philip and I had little or nothing in common; and we soon found each other's society very tame. In spite of me, my heart was hungry, and I am afraid that I never really set myself to make Philip happy. To make matters worse, Robert and Maggie, not knowing of our whereabouts, came and settled in the same suburb. The gold rush was over, and Robert had obtained employment in the city. At first we thought of leaving the district, or, at least, of ignoring them; but we were both bored and wretched, and any new interest seemed attractive. Moreover, I saw Robert pass the window several times without his knowledge, and I thought that he bore a great burden. His face was heavy and sad and, I fancied, regretful. Perhaps we ought to have acted on our first impulse and moved away without their knowing of our presence there. Perhaps the very hunger of my heart should have warned me. All my soul was crying out for Robert and I thought that his was crying out for me. We let the weeks go by; we met, as it was inevitable that we should; and we spent many of our evenings at each other's homes.

'The position—always bad—quickly became intolerable. Philip saw the truth; how could he help it? Maggie saw the truth; how could she help it? And, to complicate matters still further, Philip and Maggie were drawn to each other. They seemed made for each other; Maggie had the gaiety and sparkle for which Philip pined; I was like a millstone round his neck. Philip had all the qualities that appealed to Maggie. So there we were! The very reasons that should have kept us all apart drew us all together. We were always at their home or they at ours. And the more we met them, and they us, the more hideous our unhappiness became.'

Mary paused for a moment in her story, and she nervously brushed away the apple-petals that had fallen on her lap. When she was mistress of herself once more, she continued:

'It was Philip who brought things to a head. Poor Philip! He deserved to be happy, and I was ashamed of the misery I had brought him. He was always dashing and impulsive, and, one evening, without saying a word to me, he went off by himself. He returned about supper-time.

'"Look here, Mary," he said, as soon as he sat down, "we can't go on like this. We've all done wrong—except Maggie. I've been round and had a talk with Robert. We've agreed, if you and Maggie are willing, to part. Maggie and I will go back to the Old Country. Robert says that, if you consent, he will go with you to New Zealand. We shall start life afresh, with a better chance of being happy."

'It was wrong, very wrong,' Mary continued, 'but I agreed. Philip and Maggie went back to England; settled down near Manchester, prospered in business, were very happy, and had several children. One of the boys recently came out and went on to a sheep station in Taranaki. Robert and I were happy, too, in a way. We went farming; we made money quickly and were very comfortable. No children came to our home; but we were very fond of each other—very fond—to the last.' Mary paused and brushed her eyes with her apron.

'But you know,' she went on, 'in these country districts the church is the centre of everything. At first Robert and I hesitated about attending church. We felt that we should like to; all our traditions pointed that way. And we felt that we ought to. Moreover, our consistent absence without giving a reason would cause comment and demand explanation. And yet—what of our secret?

'We decided to go; we never joined; never attended Communion; and, although Robert was highly respected, and was constantly urged to accept office, he never did so. Then we began to ask ourselves why. As the church became more and more dear to us, our consciences troubled us increasingly. We were everything to each other; we would rather die than part; and yet——it grew upon us that our relationship was a defiance of all the laws of man and God. The fact that it excluded us from life's most sacred things made us feel how wrong it was. We were like the lepers, who, outside the city walls, cried continually: "Unclean! Unclean!"

'Yet what could we do? To confess our guilt would be to shatter the happiness of Maggie and Philip, to dishonour their names and to cast a slur upon their children. We decided—God alone knows what it cost us!—to right the wrong, so far as it was in our power to do so, by separating. We sold the farm; Robert went to live in town; at my request he bought me this cottage; and we pledged ourselves never to meet again. It was a sore, sore parting——'

She again hid her face in her apron. There was a long pause. When she looked up there was a light in her countenance that I shall never forget. She seemed suddenly transfigured.

'*Perhaps*,' she said, turning full upon me, '*perhaps it will all be put right when we meet again. But I wanted you to know. You will understand now why I never joined the church. And sometimes, when you are talking to the young men and maidens in your congregation, you will be able to tell them that because in all the wide, wide world, there is nothing so beautiful as love, it is a bitter, bitter thing to tamper with it when it comes. If only Robert and I had been true to our love from the first———!'*

Poor Mary! the sun was getting low, so I took her arm and walked with her into the cottage. She grew rapidly feebler and, within the year, followed Robert into the land where all life's tangles are unravelled. And, in arranging for her funeral, I took care that, in death at least, he and she were not divided.

V

BLIND ALLEYS

I

A blind alley is an ugly monument to somebody's stupidity. Some one has blundered. No thoroughfare ought to end in a brick wall. Every street should lead into another. Every pathway should be a link in an endless chain. Every step that a man takes should bring him nearer the capital or nearer the ocean, nearer the heart of things or nearer the fringe of things, nearer the centre or nearer the circumference. Every man on the march should be able to congratulate himself on the things that he is leaving and on the things he is approaching. Every traveller is entitled to the inspiration that arises from the lengthening road behind him and the dwindling distance before. A blind alley murders all such enthusiasms. In Plato's Ideal Republic there were no blind alleys. In Sir Thomas More's Utopia there were no blind alleys. In the Citie Faire there is no blind alley to be found. In the New Jerusalem that cometh down out of heaven from God, every road leads somewhere. Every thoroughfare is a highway to infinity.

II

Today, however, we are dealing, not with dreams, but with realities. We are concerned, not with things as they *should* be—and *will* be; but with things as they actually *are*. We are living in a world that, every now and again, ensnares us in a blind alley. We come to a point that is not our destination, yet beyond which progress is impossible. We come to an end that is no end. It is an artificial and unnatural end, an end that intervenes between ourselves and our ultimate goal. There is no finality about it. It is like coming to the last page of an engrossing book only to find that it is one of three volumes, and that the other two are unobtainable. In some cases it may be worse. 'I have a horror of blind alleys,' writes my friend, Hubert Cransford. Mr. Cransford is the father of a number of boys. As they have developed towards youth and manhood, he has been singularly successful in introducing each of them to a trade or profession in which there was ample scope for the play of his personality and the gratification of his ambition. 'One is so tempted,' the father writes, 'to grasp at a comfortable and remunerative position without noticing that it leads to nothing. It is a blind alley, that is all!' Many a man, snared in such a cul-de-sac, has testified bitterly to the wretchedness of it. At the best it is like coming to the end of the odd volume of a novel; and at the *worst* it resembles being caught like a rat in a trap. At first blush it may seem that there is no analogy. For, when the rat is startled by hearing the door of the trap crash down behind him, he can go neither forward nor backward. He is in an alley that is blind at both ends! No man, it may be argued, is quite as unfortunate. And yet, in point of fact, the two situations are more similar than they at first appear. For, by the time a man discovers his mistake, he often feels that life is too far spent to permit of a fresh beginning. He is too disheartened to retrace his steps. He feels that it is too late to start all over again. He looks wistfully back at the far end of the alley—the end by which he entered it—but it ends in looking back. He does not go back. And if, by some legerdemain, a door like the door of the rat-trap were to block up that distant entrance, and cut off his retreat, it would not add in the slightest degree to his misery.

Civilization is riddled with blind alleys. The prosperity that ends in my being prosperous is a blind alley; the education that ends in my being educated is a blind alley; the amusement that ends in my being amused is a blind alley; the religion that ends in my being religious is a blind alley. These broad highways were never intended to end abruptly at the points that I have indicated. My prosperity, instead of ending with the inflation of my bank account, should lead to the enrichment of the world. My education, instead of ending with a university triumph, should equip my whole individuality for loftier service. My amusement, instead of being a mere revel, should be a tonic, a refreshment, a recreation. And my religion, instead of merely filling my soul with a smug and unwholesome self-content, should help every man I meet to fight life's battle with a braver heart. Life's great felicities were intended, not for my intoxication, but for my exhilaration. Every good and perfect gift was designed as a means to an end. It was designed, that is to say, to lead me on to something better still. It is an open road. And, whenever I wilfully block and barricade one of these thoroughfares, so that, instead of its being a means to an end, it becomes an end in itself I maliciously convert the king's highway into a blind alley, and the world is a poorer place in consequence.

III

Every man who does a thing for the sake of doing it is in a blind alley. In his *Woman in White*, Mr. Wilkie Collins has described Sir Percival Glyde. Sir Percival occupied all his time, when he was alone, in cutting walking-sticks. The mere act of cutting and lopping, we are told, appeared to please him. He filled the house with walking-sticks of his own making, not one of which he ever took up a second time. When they were finished, his interest in them was all exhausted. And he thought of nothing but of going out and making more! He made walking-sticks for the sake of making walking-sticks. He is in a blind alley, and he is not alone.

If you look carefully into that blind alley of his, you will see a great number of people wandering aimlessly up and down it. They are all people who are doing things for the mere sake of doing things. Here is the man who speaks, not because he has something to say, but because he feels that he ought to say something. The man who talks for the sake of talking; the man who sings for the sake of singing; and, worst of all, the man who preaches for the sake of preaching; they are all in Sir Percival Glyde's blind alley. The man who makes money for the mere sake of making money is very near of kin to the man who makes walking-sticks for the mere sake of making walking-sticks. When these people retrace their steps, leave the blind alley behind them, and find their feet on life's broad highroad, it will be an immense addition to their own happiness and an immense aug-mentation of the public good.

IV

In surveying the heavens on a starry night, I like to remind myself that God does not make worlds as Sir Percival Glyde makes walking-sticks. He does not make them for the fun of making them. In His vast creative programme, He is on an open thoroughfare, not in a blind alley. He is working, with sublime patience and infinite skill, towards the

> . . . one far-off divine event
> To which the whole creation moves.

On any theory of the universe the life that is implies a greater life to be. There are those who think that, in calling His worlds into being, God created first *this* and then *that* and then *the other*. That being so, it is inconceivable that God brought all these wonders into existence that He might litter His universe with worlds as Sir Percival Glyde littered his walls with walking-sticks. Again, there are those who think that, for countless ages, the Most High has been marshalling an orderly and intricate and sublime process of evolution. But they, too, feel that, if all this ends in itself, it is a blind alley. Moreover, they feel—cannot help feeling—that it does *not* end in itself. In his classic on *Immortality*, Professor A. W. Momerie points out that, 'in the process of evolution, we find distinct evidences of a meaning, a purpose, a plan, of what Professor Fiske has well called *a dramatic tendency*.'

And, a little further on, he says again that 'the more thoroughly we comprehend the process of evolution, the more fully convinced shall we be that it is throughout a rational process, and that therefore it cannot come to an irrational conclusion, cannot end in an anti-climax. The more thoroughly we comprehend the process of evolution, the more profoundly shall we feel that to deny the immortality of the soul is to rob the whole process of its meaning. To suppose that what has been evolved at such cost will suddenly collapse is to convert the mighty drama of creation into an imbecile and drivelling farce. Immortality is the only possible climax to that creative work which has been, in all its myriad stages, so wonderful so divine.'

Darwin himself said as much. He felt, and felt acutely, that the evolution that led to extinction was a blind alley. 'Believing as I do,' he wrote, 'that man in the distant future will be a far more perfect creature than he now is, it is an intolerable thought that he is doomed to complete annihilation after such long-continued progress. To those who fully admit the immortality of the human soul, the destruction of our world will not appear so dreadful.' We may interpret the phenomena about us as we will, and account for their existence as we may; but, on any theory, man is out on the open road. He is in no blind alley. He is going somewhere. He is a pilgrim of eternity.

V

We have all felt the pathos of the snapped columns that are so often erected to commemorate lives that, broken suddenly, seemed sadly incomplete. From the waters of one of our Australian rivers—the Parramatta—there rises a tall but broken column to the memory of a young oarsman—Henry Earnest Searle—who, after winning the championship of the world, died at the age of twenty-one. And, within walking distance of this quiet study of mine, is a broken column to which every year thousands of people pay pilgrimage. It marks the resting-place of Adam Lindsay Gordon, the poet of our vast Australian solitudes:

> A shining soul with syllables of fire
> Who sang the first great songs these lands can claim.

He was little more than a boy in years, and he was altogether a boy in spirit, when his light was suddenly extinguished. I select these two instances, almost at random, and because on these expressive monuments my own eyes have so often rested. The symbol is very common; and it is common for the simple reason that the poignant problem that it symbolizes is so common. Let Principal Fairbairn state it. 'Here,' he says,' is a young man full of promise. He has been a bright and happy boy, the pride of his mother's heart, the light of his father's eye; he has been an earnest student, the joy of his tutors, the hope of his school and his college, raising high expectations even in the withered breast of his professor. He has been the centre of a brilliant circle of friends, who talked with him, walked with him, disputed and argued with him concerning high things, ever stimulated by his brilliant thought and vivid speech. He comes to the threshold of life, with school and university behind him, high hopes and fair visions before him, and noble purposes looking out from his radiant face. And, just then, a fatal disease claims him as its own; and he dies, while men whose hearts are dry as summer dust linger on in what they call life.'

Every man who lets his memory roam for a minute among the old familiar faces of his school and college days will find it easy to fill out this general outline with personal detail. In his *Life of Richard Jefferies*, who died at thirty-eight, Edward Thomas marvels that Jefferies was permitted to drop into his grave just as he was beginning to find himself and to see life whole. And a later writer, singularly enough, has made a similar remark concerning Edward Thomas himself! 'What a mystery it is,' says Canon Ainger, in a letter to Mrs. Bowles concerning the death of her young brother,' what a mystery it is that a life should be taken just when it has been receiving and was about to begin bearing fruit!' It is indeed! These gallant young souls were just getting into their stride when they found themselves confronted by an apparently impassable barrier. It really looks as if we have found a blind alley at last.

VI

But have we? Or is it only an illusion? There are several answers. The first is that these brief lives, apparently broken, are not as incomplete as they appear. Let us return to Principal Fairbairn. The Principal turns abruptly from philosophy to autobiography. He speaks of an early comrade of his own. They were more than brothers to each other. They lived, they thought, they argued together; together they walked on the hillside and by the sea-shore; together they listened to the wind as it soughed through the trees and to the multitudinous laughter of the waves as they broke upon the beach; together they watched the purple light which floated radiant above the heather, and together they descended into the slums of a great city, where no light was, nor any fragrance, and faced the worst depravity of our time. Each kept hope alive in the other, and stimulated him to high endeavour and better purpose; but though the same week saw the two friends settled in chosen fields of labour, the one settled only to be called home, the other to remain and work his tale of toil until his longer day should close. 'But,' adds the Principal, 'the one who died seemed to leave his spirit behind in the breast of the man who survived: and he has lived ever since, and lives still, feeling as if the soul within him belongs to the man who passed away.' It is a thought worth thinking.

And here is another! Highways often masquerade. They pretend to be blind alleys. It is only when the traveller reaches the end that he sees the way out. A few weeks ago, in a small boat, I was making my way up one of the most picturesque of our Australian rivers. The forestry on both banks was magnificent beyond description, and every twig was most exquisitely mirrored in the glassy waters below. A canoe glided ahead of us. Presently the waters seemed to come to an end. As we shaded our eyes with our hands, and surveyed the prospect in front of us, it looked as if we had reached the head of a lake. Our progress appeared to be barred. We watched the canoe, and, to our astonishment, it simply vanished! The banks seemed to swallow it up. We rowed on; and, when we came to the point at which the canoe had so mysteriously disappeared, we beheld a sudden twist in the river artfully concealed by the tangle of bush. The blind alley was no blind alley after all! These young pilgrims, whose names we have inscribed upon our broken columns, have gone on

—like the canoe. It had turned a bend in the river: they have turned a bend in the road.

It was Victor Hugo who declared with splendid passion that, neither for youth nor for age, is a tomb a blind alley. He was himself old. 'But I feel,' he exclaimed, 'that I have not said a thousandth part of what is in me. When I go down to the grave, I can say, like so many others, "I have finished my day's work," but I cannot say, "I have finished my life." Another day's work will begin the next morning. *My tomb is not a blind alley*, it is a thoroughfare; it closes with the twilight to open with the dawn.' It is the only explanation of the incompleteness that we see everywhere. 'Truly,' Browning makes Paracelsus cry:

> Truly there needs another life to come!
> If this be all—. . .
> And other life await us not—for one
> I say 'tis a poor cheat, a stupid bungle,
> A wretched failure. I, for one, protest
> Against it, and I hurl it back with scorn.

If that were so, we should all be caught in a blind alley. The Great Artist would have begun a picture which He had not the skill to finish. The Great Father would have given His children a promise which was beyond His power to keep.

VII

The New Testament contains a tragic story of a man who regarded the world in which he lived not as a means to an end, but as an end in itself. 'Soul,' he said, 'thou hast much goods laid up for many years! Take thine ease; eat, drink, and be merry!' With his wealthy accumulation of goods he blocked the king's highway and turned it into a blind alley. The barricade that he had built stood at last between himself and heaven. He turned the highway into an alley and lost his soul in the process.

VI

PHOEBE'S PERPLEXITY

I

'Phoebe Dryden wants you in the study, father! She seems dreadfully upset about something or other.'

To the study I accordingly hastened; and, as I had been given to expect, found poor Phoebe very agitated and perturbed. Dressed in a becoming brown costume, she sat in the big study arm-chair, her muff on her lap, her fur thrown lightly about her shoulders, a letter in one hand and her gloves in the other.

'I don't know what to do,' she exclaimed plaintively, as soon as I was seated. 'I received this invitation from Katie Milligan yesterday—you know Katie; you remember meeting her at our place on the night of Gerald's party—and I've been in trouble about it ever since. Mother and Hettie think I ought to go; and, really, I don't know what Katie will think of me if I don't. But father says that he was never allowed to go to anything of the kind. I showed the invitation to Mr. Bellamy, who takes our

Sunday afternoon Bible Class; and he says that I certainly ought to decline it. What do you think?'

Poor little Phoebe! As she sat there, the picture of misery, her pretty face turned pleadingly towards me, I felt very sorry for her. I felt sorry, too, for Katie Milligan. She is a nice girl, overflowing with life and merriment; she had made an honest attempt to give Phoebe pleasure; and *this* was the measure of her success!

What was it, you ask, to which Katie had invited her friend? That, if you please, is *Katie's* business!

Did Phoebe accept or decline the invitation? That is *Phoebe's* business.

How did I advise her? That is *my* business!

But the general principles involved? They are *everybody's* business. It is with them, therefore, that I propose to deal.

II

Laughter, merriment, and fun were quite evidently intended to occupy a large place in this world. Yet on no subject under the sun has the Church displayed more embarrassment and confusion. One might almost suppose that here we have discovered an important phase of human experience on which Christianity is criminally reticent; a *terra incognita* which no intrepid prophet had explored; a silent sea upon whose waters no ecclesiastical adventurer had ever burst; a dark and eerie country upon which no sun had ever shone. Dr. Jowett tells us of the devout old Scotsman who, on Saturday night, locked up the piano and unlocked the organ, reversing the process last thing on the Sabbath evening. The piano is the sinner; the organ the saint! Dr. Parker used to wax merry at the man who regarded bagatelle as a gift from heaven, whilst billiards he deemed to be a stepping-stone to perdition.

The play we condemn; it is anathema to us. The same play—or a vastly inferior one—screened on a film, we delightedly admire. One Christian follows the round of gaiety with the maddest of the merry; another wears a hair shirt, and starves himself into a skeleton. One treats life as all a frolic; another as all a funeral. We swerve from the Scylla of aestheticism to the Charybdis of asceticism. We swing like the pendulum from the indulgence of the Epicurean to the severities of the Stoic, failing to recognize, with the author of *Ecce Homo*, that it is the glory of Christianity that, rejecting the absurdities of each, it combines the cardinal excellences of both. We allow without knowing why we allow; we ban without knowing why we prohibit. We

> Compound for sins we are inclined to
> By damning those we have no mind to.

We are at sea without chart or compass. Our theories of pleasure are in hopeless confusion. Is there no definite doctrine of amusement? Is there no philosophy of fun? There must be! And there is!

III

Gideon was the first man to state the doctrine clearly. His army is approaching the valley in which the Arab host lies encamped. The stream separates them from the foe. For aught they know, the reeds and rushes of that stream may be alive with ambushed Midianites. It is an hour for a quick eye and a cool head. But, in that hour, some of the men so far forget their soldierly duties as to lie down, with a fearful abandon, and drink of the stream, rendering their necks an easy prey to a hidden sword. These men Gideon dismissed, taking with him only those who, vigilant and alert, watching as they walk and walking as they watch, dip up water in their hands to refresh and recreate them. The application is obvious. If I dip up my pleasure as I press on, and in order to give me new zest and energy in pressing on, my pleasure is good. I simply enjoy it:

> As the rider that rests with the spur on his heel—
> As the guardsman that sleeps in his corselet of steel.

But if, on the contrary, my pleasure necessitates a period of abandonment—a distinct interval and parenthesis aside from, and inconsistent with, my main character and duty—then I can only indulge it by hazarding my fidelity, as did Gideon's men, and I shall be counted unworthy.

There is nothing wrong, I see, about the stream; nor in the men drinking of the stream. Even warriors weary, and must be refreshed. The evil is in the manner and the extent of their indulgence. That is surely what John Bunyan means when he writes of the arbour at the summit of the Hill Difficulty. As a place of rest and refreshment for tired pilgrims, it was as welcome and as providential as Gideon's stream; but Christian never forgave himself for having slept and lost his roll in the hospice which the Prince of the Pilgrims had provided for his recreation. Vinet says that every enjoyment too much indulged impoverishes us spiritually, and he can understand that it might be said, 'That armchair has kept in its cushions a portion of my soul!' That is the doctrine according to Gideon.

IV

David was the second man to state the doctrine clearly. At risk of their lives three valiant men fought their way through the ranks of the enemy, and brought David the water, from the old well at Bethlehem, for which his soul had longed. But, when they brought it, the water seemed to turn crimson in the cup. It was like drinking blood of the men who had hazarded their lives to obtain it. And he poured it our upon the ground. David's is a somewhat searching test. It clearly concerned a matter of pleasure. It was not a matter of necessity arising from thirst, or *any* water would have satisfied him, the clear water seemed as red as blood before his eyes. He would not drink of it. And all ages have admired his stern refusal.

Here, then, is a standard to which I may safely submit my pleasures. I have no right to enjoy a pleasure that can only be had at the risk of another man's life. That is a principal capable of very wide application. If a proposed pastime will not satisfactorily pass the ordeal of this crucible, it is, at any rate, safer to abjure it. Life consists not in self-indulgence, but in self-denial.

Balzac has given us the fable of the Magic Skin. He who wore it possessed the power to obtain anything he craved, but, every time he availed himself of that mysterious power, the skin shrank and compressed him, until at length it crushed his very life out. Some particular performances are often very plausibly defended on the ground that they minister to the highest instincts of the aesthetic and the beautiful. But David's test shows that there is another aspect of the question to be considered before the case is complete. The performance may be the finest fun in the world to the audience; but it may be a tragedy worse than a thousand murders to the performers. And if that be so, the Church has her doctrine clear-cut and imperative. That is the doctrine according to David.

V

Solomon was the third man to state the doctrine clearly. The wise man, who perhaps bought much of his wisdom dearly, puts the case unmistakably. Here it is: '*Hast thou found honey? Eat so much as is sufficient for thee, lest thou be filled therewith and vomit it.*' First of all, that is to say, make sure you have found honey. It must be not only sweet, but pure, nutritious, natural, wholesome. It must neither injure nor besmirch. Sophronius, according to the old story, had a fair daughter named Eulalia. She came to him one day and asked his permission to visit the gay Lucinda. The father regretfully, but firmly, forbade it.

'You must think me very weak!' retorted the daughter petulantly; 'in what way would it hurt me to go?'

Sophronius picked a dead coal from the hearth and held it towards Eulalia. She hesitated to accept it.

'Take it, my child,' he said, 'it will not burn you!'

'It may not *burn*,' she replied, 'but it will *blacken*!' And, even as she uttered the words, she saw their parabolic significance, the significance which had moved her father to his strange action.

There is a sense in which the pleasures that blacken are worse than the pleasures that burn. A burned hand will not burn the hand that it clasps; but a blackened hand will spread broadcast its defilement.

Pleasure must be recreation, or it fails of its purpose. 'If,' said Dr. Arnold, whose religion was of so robust a type that he made a thousand school-boys almost worship him, 'if your pleasures are such that they prejudice your next day's duties; if they are such that the main business and interest of life suffer in consequence, they are not pleasures—they are revellings!' Make sure, says Solomon, that you have found honey. The pathetic aspect of much of our modern pleasure-seeking is that men and women who earn and richly deserve pleasure fail to find it, simply for lack of observing Solomon's advice. They are, as Cowper would say:

> Letting down buckets into empty wells,
> And growing old with drawing nothing up.

The tragedy of the age is, not that people are getting too much pleasure, but that they are not getting enough. The appetite is jaded; the soul is blasé. The halls of amusement are thronged by eager multitudes in the frantic quest of pleasure; yet it is notorious that a really satisfying delight is only occasionally found there.

It is clear, then, that an application of the doctrine according to Solomon would save men and women from many a fruitless quest. Make sure that you have found honey! And, says the sage, even if you are certain that you have found it, eat only as much as is sufficient for your recreation, '*lest you be filled therewith and vomit it.*' We are told that, in France, where tons of the loveliest flowers are piled in heaps for the production of perfumeries, the girls engaged in the manufacture suffer from a peculiar disease induced by the volume of fragrance which they perpetually inhale. Even if the pleasure be wholesome and pure, beware of excess. You can have too much even of a good thing. That is the doctrine according to Solomon.

VI

Petronius dreamed a dream. He was chasing Pleasure. He hunted her up hill and down dale, but could not clutch her skirts. He gave up the chase in despair. And lo, as he abandoned it, he saw One approaching him with marks of wounds in His hands and in His feet, and with scars as of thorns on His brow. '*My ways are ways of pleasantness,*' He said, '*and all My paths are peace!*' And he took the

Stranger's hand and they walked together. And, as they walked, Pleasure returned and took his other hand, and he found that, by yielding to the persuasions of the Christ, he had obtained the company of Pleasure too. And Petronius awoke, and learned by long and happy experience that the dream that he had dreamed was true.

VII

ON SWALLOWING FAGGOTS CROSSWISE

'You will have to learn to *swallow faggots crosswise*!' said the veteran to the raw recruit. The raw recruit, as it happens, was Charles Haddon Spurgeon; the veteran was an old Cambridgeshire minister to whom he had confided his intention of entering the ministry. The words clung to Mr. Spurgeon as long as he lived. Words spoken under such circumstances usually do.

I went one day to consult an old doctor. As I sat in the waiting-room his door opened, and, to my surprise, a young fellow whom I had known some years before as a medical student, came out. He greeted me cordially.

'It does a fellow good to have a talk with the old boy,' he exclaimed, not disrespectfully. 'I was going to try a scheme on one of my patients, thinking that it was brand new and startlingly original; but I find that our old friend here tried it thirty years ago. It didn't come up to expectations, it seems, but it led him to a line of action that brought a cure and he has given me one or two excellent wrinkles.' He hurried off on the best of terms with himself. A few minutes later the nurse in attendance called my name.

'Ah,' exclaimed the old man, genially, 'you've caught me in a good humour. Young Winterton has just been in. It does an old man a world of good to keep in touch with these young sparks. He was telling me of some of the latest experiments he saw in Edinburg——'; and so on. I could see that the conversation between the two doctors had been a source of delight and inspiration to both of them. Each felt as if he had caught a breath from the hills. So was it in the case that I have cited. Mr. Spurgeon never forgot the veteran's quaint remark, and, although I have no data to go upon, I am absolutely certain that, for some time after the interesting and enthusiastic youth had left the house, the old man sat chuckling and rubbing his hands, his face all wreathed in smiles and sunshine.

'A minister!' exclaimed the old man, warningly, 'you are going to be a minister! Well, well, Charles, you will have to learn to *swallow faggots crosswise!*'

I am not sure that the expressive phrase will bear a very searching examination; like so many of our proverbs and epigrams, the saying must be judged, not by the actual words that it contains, but by the impression that it conveys. I see quite clearly what the good man means; and the speaker who can effectively communicate his meaning, whether by accurate or inaccurate terminology, is not to be despised. I have known men use the most exquisitely polished phrases and leave their hearers in a state of abject mystification. 'It was very beautiful,' they say, as they make their way back to their homes, '*but what on earth did he mean?*'

Young Spurgeon was in no such perplexity as he left the old minister's house. The veteran's meaning was as plain as a pike-staff—which, as everybody knows, is the plainest of all plain things. He meant, not that a minister must *swallow faggots crosswise*, but that he must acquire the habit of so turning with his tongue the faggots that are placed crosswise in his teeth, that he will be able to swallow them with the utmost ease. And, seeing that he makes his meaning so perfectly clear, I frankly forgive everything else. Besides, if the makers of our poetry shelter themselves behind *poetic licence*, why should not the makers of our proverbs shelter themselves behind *proverbial licence?* So be it then! The old man leaves the court without a stain upon his character.

I wonder what suggested the strange expression to his mind. But why should I wonder? Let me hazard a conjecture! I have already conjured up a picture of the old man as his daughter saw him after his young visitor had gone. Why should I not indulge in a similar flight of fancy as to the things that happened before his visitor arrived? I have a notion that he knew that young Spurgeon was coming. In the nature of the case, it is not likely to have been a chance call. An appointment was almost certainly made. The old gentleman knows that, in an hour's time, a young fellow is coming to seek his advice about entering the ministry. Very well! What more natural than that he should allow his mind to play around those classical sentences that every minister so often ponders—the sentences in which the first great ministerial charge was uttered? '*Behold, I send you forth as sheep in the midst of wolves; be ye therefore wise as serpents and harmless as doves*,' and so on. A phrase like this naturally sets the old man thinking.

'*As wise as serpents!*' What can it mean? Are serpents wise? And, if so, in what does their wisdom consist? In a word, *What has a minister to learn from a snake*? The old man is perplexed, and I can sympathize with him in his perplexity. I have never yet seen a satisfactory exposition of the passage. The commentators are, obviously, all at sea. In an oracular kind of way, they make a few sagacious remarks upon the passage; but they leave you exactly where they found you. They look upon the serpent with his glittering coils, his forked tongue, his cruel fangs, his flattened head and his wicked little bead-like eyes, and they try to regard him as a ministerial model; but it is never a success. I am not surprised, therefore, at the old gentleman's bewilderment.

'*As wise as serpents!*' he says to himself, wrinkling his brows as he repeats it. '*As wise as serpents!*' And then he suddenly remembers that, among a lot of old books that, years ago, he bought at a sale, there is a volume that may throw some light on the troublesome problem. After careful search he espies the dusty old tome slumbering—as it has slumbered for years untold—on the very topmost shelf. But how is he to get it? He sees a huge faggot lying in the garden just under his window. If it were only inside he could clamber on it and reach down the book! He calls his daughter; she jumps on a chair; takes down the volume and, woman-like, dusts it; whereupon he settles down to its perusal.

'*As wise as serpents!*' he murmurs again. In what way can a minister sit at the feet of a snake, if that is to say, a snake had feet? He opens the volume; it is *Rogers on Reptiles.* He turns to the chapter on Serpents. Snakes, Mr. Rogers tells him, are of the order of vertebrates; but the spine is so delicate, so pliant and so extremely fragile that it is easily fractured. No clue as yet; it will never do to suggest to the young minister that *backbone* is a non-essential. Snakes, our learned author goes on to say, are possessed of brains so small that many eminent authorities have regarded them as altogether brainless. Still no clue. The old man reads on; he notes the conical teeth, the lidless eyes, the innumerable ribs, and all the other oddities of the hideous creatures; but he can find nothing that he can conscientiously commend to the emulation of the youth who will shortly enjoy his company. At length, however, he comes upon this: '*The digestive system includes a distensible gullet. Many serpents subsist on prey much thicker than themselves. They are able to swallow it by reason of the fact that the throat and body are capable of great dilation.*' The old gentleman thinks that this aspect of serpentine nature is worth pondering. He lays *Rogers on Reptiles* on the table; takes off his glasses and places them carefully on the open book; and then lies back in the chair to think things over.

The exertion has, however, been too much for him. His eyes close; his head nods gently once or twice; and then he drops into a peaceful sleep. And in his sleep he dreams. He dreams that in one respect at least, he is as wise as the serpent at last. He, too, has a *distensible gullet*; *his throat and body are capable of almost infinite dilation!* He can swallow anything! He swallows *Rogers on Reptiles*—reptiles and all! He swallows the chair on which his daughter stood! He swallows the table on which he laid his book and spectacles! He swallows the faggot under the window and swallows it crosswise! And, then, just as he is about to attempt a still more prodigious feat, he awakes with a start to find his daughter ushering the chubby-cheeked young Spurgeon into his room. And it was with this grotesque and fantastic vision in mind—always provided that my flight of fancy has the sanction of historical accuracy—that the old gentleman gave to the ruddy youth the sage counsel that, to his dying day, that distinguished youth never forgot.

'Well, well, Charles,' he said, 'so you are going to be a minister! You will have to learn to *swallow faggots crosswise!*'

It was excellent advice. A distensible gullet is an absolutely essential item in a ministerial outfit. I do not mean that a minister is called upon to perform greater gastronomic feats than other people. That may or may not be so; I do not know. Most people have at times to swallow extremely awkward things, and no man is the worse for a little elasticity in the region of the throat. The man who, on occasion, can gulp down a faggot or two, and smile as they descend into his dilatable interior, is likely to live to a hearty old age. I have known many a man lose a night's rest through his inability to swallow something or other; but *Rogers on Reptiles* points out, with a good deal of perspicacity, that, after swallowing a creature greater than itself, a distended serpent will go away and sleep for an indefinite period. That is a fact in natural history which is worth the careful attention of all those unfortunate mortals who are troubled with chronic, or even occasional, insomnia.

The minister is not called upon to swallow more—or bigger—faggots than the butcher, the baker, or the candlestick-maker. It is as well that he should remind himself of this important circumstance when he finds himself wrestling with a particularly unsavoury mouthful, or when the jagged edges of the faggot persist in sticking in his throat. The old gentleman's sage counsel is particularly applicable to the minister's case, however, for the simple but sufficient reason that greater interests may be jeopardized by *his* refusal to gulp the unshapely comestible. The doctor has some very awkward things said to him at times; but he finds it best to smile and pass on. The draper has to endure a good deal at the hands of his customers; but he quickly discovers that his truest wisdom—the wisdom of the serpent—the wisdom of the distensible gullet—lies in saying: 'Certainly, madam!' or 'We shall attend to that, miss!' and in letting it go at that. He swallows it!

But anybody can see at a glance why the old gentleman in Cambridgeshire lays special stress upon his quaint counsel in addressing a young minister. If his wise words apply, as they certainly do, to doctors and drapers, they apply very much more pointedly to ministers. For, if the doctor or the draper find themselves unable to gulp down the unappetizing indignities that are offered them, nobody suffers but themselves. The doctor is perfectly free to tell his querulous patient that, if he thinks that he understands his ailment better than his medical adviser, he had better write out the prescription himself. In which case the patient replies with something equally unpalatable, and they part—forever. The draper is quite at liberty to tell his fastidious customer that he is tired to death of her freaks and foibles. But, if he does so, it will simply mean that she will darken the door of his shop no more. The doctor will have lost a good patient, and the draper a good customer—that is all. But if the *minister* develops a too rigid and inflexible gullet, he may shatter the tranquillity and wreck the prosperity of an entire congregation. Men are but mortal. (I have heard it whispered that the same is true even of women!) They say and do the most awkward things, never meaning the things that they say and do to be as awkward as they seem—and are. It is so easy to stiffen the gullet and refuse to swallow. 'I shall report this to the officers!' 'I shall lay this matter before the church!' 'I shall resign!' Hoity-toity! What a pity! Why not relax the gullet just a little, and *swallow it*?

I sometimes recall an experience which marked my early days at Mosgiel. We had in the congregation a tall, angular woman, of expressionless face, who prided herself on her perfect candour. Like most people of that type, she often made remarks that stuck in the throat like faggots swallowed crosswise. One Wednesday evening, as I stood at the door to shake hands with the people who had attended the mid-week service, this woman made a remark that brought all my blood to my cheek. On my way home, I confided my vexation to one of the good old men who served on the diaconate of the church. He only laughed.

'Oh, take no notice of it,' he said. 'She means well: she says ugly things: but she wouldn't hurt you for worlds.'

Although it was early, I went straight to bed. I wanted to be alone. But it is one thing to go to bed and quite another thing to go to sleep. At last, in desperation, I got up and went for a walk. It was fairly late by this time; but there was a light in the kitchen window of the cottage in which my angular friend lived. Something prompted me to go across. I heard a heavy tread within. I tapped at the door. Her son answered my knock.

'Mother's just gone out,' he said. 'Mrs. Ardmore's baby is very ill and mother has gone to sit up with it. She said that Mrs. Ardmore had had no sleep this week, and it was time she went to bed.'

Now I had known of the child's serious sickness: I had called and inquired and spoken consolingly and hopefully to the mother. But it had never occurred to *me* to ask if there was anything that I could do to make the poor woman's long vigil more tolerable. This angular woman with the clumsy tongue had, however, hurried to the exhausted mother's succour. I chatted with the boy for a minute or two, and then returned to my bed and slept like a top. And, during the years that followed —years that brought to the manse heavy troubles and great anxieties—the woman who nursed the sick baby on that memorable night was one of our most constant comforters. The thought of her has often saved me in a moment of peril. During a ministry that is now getting fairly extensive I have never once seen trouble caused through a throat being too distensible; but, again and again, I have seen the inflexible gullet inflict upon its owner, and upon everybody else, incalculable misery.

PART II

I

SWEETHEARTS AND FIDDLESTICKS

Sweethearts and Fiddlesticks! The conjunction, I frankly admit, is a most unfortunate one; but happily I am not responsible for that. The whole trouble arises out of the fact that Miss Penelope Betteredge kept a diary. Penelope, as everybody knows, is one of the most charming and lovable characters in the greatest detective-story ever written. In gathering up the evidence by means of which he threw such a flood of light upon the famous Moonstone mystery, her father, old Gabriel Betteredge, found himself at a loss for dates. He distinctly remembered that certain things happened; but when? He had the most vivid recollection of a certain remark having been made, but on precisely what evening was it uttered?

It was in this extremity that the good man's daughter came to the rescue. Her diary, she said, would supply the missing information. She was taught at school to keep an account of all her doings, and she had persevered in the habit ever since. She was sure that her diary would give the dates required; she would run upstairs and look.

Her father—being only a man—as good as hinted that it would be better still if she were to confide the diary to his keeping and thus place all the facts in his own hands. The very idea! At the bare mention of so preposterous a proposal the indignation of the dutiful and affectionate Penelope was beautiful to see.

'Hand over my journal!' she exclaimed in horrified astonishment, her eyes flashing and her face aflame. 'My journal is for my own private eye, and no living creature shall ever know what is in it but myself!' Gabriel feebly protested that young ladies should have no such secrets.

'Fiddlesticks!' exclaimed Penelope, contemptuously.

'Sweethearts!' muttered Gabriel suspiciously.

'What is the connexion between Sweethearts and Fiddlesticks?' I asked at the tea-table after reading of this outburst.

'Is it a riddle?' somebody inquired.

'Just as you like!' I answered.

'Then,' exclaimed my questioner, confidently, 'I suppose it's something to the effect that, as with a fiddle, you only get the music from a girl's life after she has been smitten by a beau!'

I am not sure this was exactly what I had in mind; but the observation opens up a fascinating field of thought; and one is tempted to stroll up and down that field at leisure. Perhaps, however, we had better leave the *fiddlesticks* at that! I am not sure that

I can contribute much to the wisdom of the world on the subject of *fiddlesticks*; but sweethearts are always worth talking about.

Now, just for once, let us begin at the beginning, and take things in their proper order. Clearly, the first thing to talk about is Miss Penelope's diary. If there had been no diary we should have had no sweethearts and no fiddlesticks. Moreover, it is at this point that Penelope fills me with remorse. I confess with shame and confusion of face that I never kept a diary. It is too late to start now. Diaries should be begun in the days of sweethearts and fiddlesticks, or, as in Penelope's case, even earlier. Lest I should ever find myself sprawling in a cradle and beginning life all over again, I am making notes of a few respects in which I could improve on my present performance. Experience ought to count for something; I should not like to think that, in playing the game a second time, I should be as clumsy as in my first attempt. And, conspicuously among those priceless memoranda, stands the admonition: 'Keep a Diary!'

My dream of a second innings is not as fantastic as it at first appears. A man goes back to his cradle the moment that his son is born. On that never to-be-forgotten day he begins life all over again. As soon as that new birth came to me, my memorandum flashed upon my memory, and I had no alternative but to be loyal to my resolution. I accordingly hastened to the nearest stationer's, bought a well-bound manuscript-book, and, on the opening page, inscribed, on behalf of the newcomer, a precise record of all the circumstances attending his birth. *'This afternoon, at half-past five o'clock, I arrived upon this planet . . .'* and so on. For ten years now, that journal has been faithfully kept; and thus my second innings is atoning to some extent for the blunders of my first. No man can afford to make the same mistake twice.

A wise little woman was Penelope Betteredge! Whether she knew it or not, she was following in the footsteps of the great masters. What an impoverishment would overtake the world if all the diaries were taken out of it! As all readers of Mr. Wilkie Collins know, Penelope's diary proved simply invaluable. It was originally written, as she so emphatically protested, for her own eyes only; but in the end it proved of inestimable benefit to every character in the tale. In that respect it was but conforming to the historic traditions of documents of the kind. Thousands of men and women have kept diaries; and have intended what they wrote for no eyes but their own It is part of our deep, deep instinct for the confessional. The soul must utter itself somewhere. Claudius Clear declares that the most remarkable diary in the English language is that of Sir Walter Scott. He began it on November 20, 1825. He was then fifty-four, and he had but seven years to live. The clouds were gathering about him; ruin stared him in the face. 'Why,' asked our essayist, 'did Scott write that journal? It was, I think, because he had to express himself, and there was no friend to whom he could tell the whole bitter truth. He could not tell it to his son-in-law, Lockhart, for he had kept Lockhart very much in the dark. The same was true of his Edinburgh friends. His wife—never much of a companion—broke down absolutely under her trial, and soon passed from the troubled scene. He was too chivalrous to burden the minds of his children with any trouble he could spare them. What is most distressing in the whole tragical yet glorious business was that Scott, the friend of all, had no friend in the day of his dire duress with whom he could be perfectly frank.' And so, a broken man, he took a paper book, made it his father-confessor, and poured out his anguished soul to it.

But the singular thing is that the diaries that were written in the first instance for only one pair of eyes, have, in the end, proved the enrichment of the world. Men like Bunyan and Wesley and Baxter were great believers in putting things down. And, as a consequence, Bunyan's *Grace Abounding*, and Wesley's *Journal*, and Baxter's *Autobiography* form part of the Church's priceless heritage. Here we have religion expressed in the terms of actual experience; there is a ring of reality about it; and we would rather lose all our philosophies and theologies than allow one of these artless but invaluable documents to perish.

Especially do I admire, in this connexion, the amazing sagacity and insight of John Wesley. Wesley believed that, like bees in amber, the soul's experiences should be embalmed for the inspection of subsequent generations. Acting upon this conviction, he not only gave us his own journal—a work that runs into thousands of printed pages— but he moved all his comrades and associates to follow his example. He encouraged Charles, his brother, to keep a record of everything. Is it not possible that to his influence we owe the journals of George Whitefield and John Fletcher?

However that may be, it is certain that Wesley required all his preachers—Nelson, Haime, Olivers, Hopper, Jaco, Mitchell, and the rest—to reduce to writing the story of their spiritual travail. Wesley was astute enough to know two things. He knew that it would do *those men* a world of good to set their experiences down, and he knew that it would do me a world of good to read what they had written. 'It was not my intention,' says John Haime, 'to write any account of these things. I put it off from time to time, being conscious that I had no talent for writing, until my peace was well-nigh lost. At last I was prevailed upon to begin. I had not written many lines before I found my soul in perfect peace!'

Precisely! John Haime's soul began to glow as soon as he began to write; and my soul caught fire as soon as I began to read. The pen was a means of grace to him; the paper was a means of grace to me. John Wesley was so astute, and so shrewd, and so far-seeing that he deliberately engineered this twofold benediction—the writer's and the reader's.

The world has never seen such a believer in diaries as John Wesley. The autobiographical literature of early Methodism is as voluminous as it is valuable. In the corner of my study there are a few shelves apart. They form a kind of chapel, or sanctuary, or shrine. I turn to them whenever I feel that the lights within are burning low, and I never turn to them in vain. I hope that I shall never have to choose between these diaries on the one hand and all the rest of the books in the library on the other; but, if I do, I am afraid that all the rest will have to go.

Gabriel thought, however, that Penelope's diary was all about sweethearting! And what if it was? Sweethearting is lovely. In one of those old journals which I have just been praising—the Journal of Christopher Hopper—I find an entry which provokes a shudder. It concerns the year 1758. Hopper was then a widower of six-and-thirty; he was young enough to know better. '*In the latter end of this year,*' he icily says, '*I had some thoughts of changing my life again. I prayed for divine direction, and took the advice of some friends. One who loved me, and wished me well, recommended to me an agreeable person of a fair character; and on April 17, 1759, we were married.'* This is the only thing in Hopper's Journal that I disliked. It smacks too much of the matrimonial advertisement.

'Recommended!'—you fancy you see a little budget of testimonials!

'An agreeable person of a fair character!'—what lover ever spoke of his sweetheart in such terms?

No, I do not like it; never did and never shall! A man may, of course, get a good wife, just as Christopher Hopper did, through the 'recommendation' of a friend, or, for that matter, through a matrimonial agency. But an ounce of real, old-fashioned sweethearting is worth a ton of this kind of thing. .

I was expressing sentiments of this kind to Arthur Baxter, who looked in just now, and he casually suggested that perhaps people didn't go in for sweethearting in Christopher Hopper's time. Didn't they? In his *Kate Carnegie*, Ian Maclaren tells a very pretty story. General Carnegie, it will be remembered, had just brought Kate home from India, and was showing her her Scottish inheritance. They walked down the glen, across the fields, through the great primrosed woods and along the banks of the laughing little trout-stream. At times their feet were buried in the wild flowers. Then, suddenly, just beside the silver water, they came upon a lonely grave! It consisted of a little square, a weather-beaten railing and a simple stone. They sat down among the hyacinths on the water's edge, and the General told Kate the deathless story. These were two sisters. During the great plague of 1666 they fled to this secluded district to escape infection; a lover came to visit one of them, and brought death in his kiss; they sickened and died and were laid to rest beside the Tochty water. And, since then, generations of lovers have made pilgrimages to this quiet spot and tenderly renewed their vows.

'He ought not to have come,' said the General. 'It was a cowardly, selfish act; but I suppose,' he added, 'he could not keep away.'

'Be sure,' replied Kate, 'she thought none the less of him for coming, and I think a woman will count life itself a small sacrifice for love.' And Kate strolled over to the grave.

A thrush was singing as they turned to go, and nothing was said on the way home till they came near the lodge.

'Father,' said Kate, 'we have seen many beautiful things today, for which I thank you, but *the greatest of these was love!*'

This was in 1666; a hundred years before Christopher Hopper; and if Arthur Baxter cares to go back a century further yet, he will come upon William Shakespeare. And William Shakespeare stands as, beyond all compare, the greatest exponent and delineator of our English sweethearting. But Arthur threw out his conjecture hastily: I feel sure that, before the click of the gate had died away, he recognized that he had made a serious mistake. Sweethearting is not the fashion of an age. I think I have already pointed out that the heathen world has nothing at all corresponding to this delicious sweethearting of ours. Men and women are thrown into each other's arms by barter, by compact, by conquest, and in a thousand ways. In one land a man buys his bride; in another he fights as the brutes do for the mate of his fancy; in yet another he takes her without seeing her, it was so ordained. Only in a land that has felt the spell of the influence of Jesus would sweethearting, as we know it, be possible. The pure and charming freedom of social intercourse; the liberty to yield to the mystic magnetism that draws the one to the other, and the other to the one; the coy approach; the shy exchanges; the arm-in-arm walks, and the heart-to-heart talks; the growing admiration; the deepening passion; culminating at last in the fond formality of the engagement and the rapture of ultimate union —in what land, unsweetened by the power of the gospel, would such a procedure be possible? Whenever I meet a pair of lovers in a leafy lane I know that I am living in a land in which church bells are constantly ringing, and in which church spires point men's hearts and minds with steadfast influence to the skies.

To sweethearting the British nation owes an incalculable debt. To vindicate that statement, I need not wander beyond that little autobiographical chapel in the corner of my study. The men who wrote those journals know what sweethearting was worth. Believe me, Christopher Hopper is quite an exceptional case. If I were to call for a volunteer to start forth as the champion of sweethearting, John Newton would leap from his shelf with the agility of a fallow deer. For John Newton had a sweetheart; and, but for that faithful little sweetheart of his, we should never have heard of John Newton. When Newton was quite a boy he fell passionately in love with Mary Catlett. Mary was only thirteen at the time—the age of Shakespeare's Juliet. During all his wild and wayward years in Africa and on the high seas, Mary's face was always before his mind. Professor Goldwin Smith, whose authority on matters of English history is absolutely final, says that 'Newton's affection for Mary Catlett was as constant as it was romantic. His father frowned on the engagement, and he became estranged from home; but through all his wanderings and sufferings he never ceased to think of her; and after seven years she became his wife. Bishop Moule, of Durham, declares that Newton's pure and passionate devotion to this simple and sensible little sweetheart of his was 'the one merciful anchor that saved him from final self-abandonment.' As the violin is silent until its soul vibrates to the touch of the bow, so Newton's life was mute, and worse than mute, until the gentle influence of Mary Catlett wooed the music from its depths.

Penelope need not, therefore, be so angry. There is no reason for her indignation and her blushes. Even if her diary is concerned with sweethearting, she need not be ashamed. More than once, sweethearting has been the making and moulding of men. As Tennyson says:

> Love took up the harp of life
> And smote on all the chords with might;
> Smote the chord of self that, trembling,
> Passed in music out of sight.

Kate Carnegie is right! She was moved by a true impulse when she surveyed from the lodge-gates the woods all twinkling with primroses and the hills all waving with bluebells. The world is full of beautiful, beautiful things, but, as she said, *the greatest of these is love.*

II

M.R.C.S.

It is, I find, very generally supposed that the letters M.R.C.S.—which so often embellish the burnished brass at a doctor's door—indicate a Member of the Royal College of Surgeons. The editor of my encyclopaedia shares with lots of really intelligent people this extraordinary conviction. It is a pretty fancy: far be it from me to attempt its demolition. So far from indulging in a fury of denial, I shall simply make a positive affirmation. The fact is that, *to me*, the letters M.R.C.S. suggest nothing in the way of surgery. To me the letters M.R.C.S. stand for *My Remarkable Collar Stud*: only that and nothing more! There, then, is my positive declaration; and, stated in that way, I doubt if it will elicit a single syllable of criticism or protest from any Member of the Royal College of Surgeons.

Now there is only one really extraordinary thing about M.R.C.S.—the collar stud, I mean, not the College of Surgeons—and you might turn it over in your hand a million times, and examine it under the most powerful microscope, without discovering its outstanding distinction. You might take it to the sharpest detective, or to the most masterly scientist, or to the most experienced jeweller, and, after scrutinizing M.R.C.S. in every conceivable way, he would utterly fail to find anything singular about it. M.R.C.S. is quite a plain affair; it has no flashing stone or scintillating gem; it possesses no secret spring or ingenious mechanism; it serves no purpose that could not be served equally well by the commonest old bone stud on the market; yet, for all that, M.R.C.S. is unquestionably entitled to the proud name it bears. For, on hot days and cold days, fine days and wet days, Sundays and week days, high days and holidays, I have worn that stud, every day, without a break, for nearly twenty years.

Stated in that way, it looks a long time; yet, viewed from another angle, the moment of my introduction to M.R.C.S. seems to me a thing of yesterday. It was at a cricket match. It was by no means a great match. Nobody enjoys a test match more than I do; but the worst of a test match is that one has to remind himself every three minutes that the earth will continue to revolve around the sun even if all his pet batsmen lose their wickets cheaply. The thing is too grimly serious to be perfectly enjoyable. But, in the match at which M.R.C.S. and I first met, there was no such intensity of concern. It was purely a friendly game between the young fellows of two government departments. It was played on one of the most picturesque grounds that

I have ever visited; the day was the perfection of early summer time; and, if the cricket was not taken as seriously as it might be, there was, by way of compensation, a delightful restfulness and sociability in the air. The players had invited their sisters and sweethearts and friends to be present; and, altogether, the afternoon passed most pleasantly.

It was not until the long shadows of the tall pine-trees began to creep across the bright sward that the cricket itself began to engross the general attention. During the early part of the day the game had been very one-sided. Then came the interval for afternoon-tea, with its opportunity for conversation and introductions. And, as soon as the match was resumed, a change came over the spirit of the dream. A young fellow went in to bat who quickly set to work to repair the fallen fortunes of his side. He cut and snicked and pulled and drove in the most masterly fashion; two or three balls in every over went to the boundary—or over it; each bowler in turn was treated with defiance and contempt. I noticed, not far from me, a little girl tremendously excited. She fairly shrieked as with stroke after stroke, the ball went bounding to the palings. I soon discovered that she was the brilliant batsman's sister; and I walked across to share her delicious glee. We had a lively hour together whilst her brother won the match for his side; and then I congratulated her and turned to go. As I shook hands with her, something in the grass at my feet caught her eye. It was M.R.C.S.! She held it up and glanced round, but nobody claimed it. 'Ah, well,' she said, laughingly, 'then you must have it; it will do to remember Vernon's score by!' She is a proud young mother now; and has, I dare say, forgotten all about the excitement of that summer evening. But it was then that M.R.C.S. came into my possession; it went on duty at the back of my neck next morning; and, day by day, has taken up its post there ever since.

I scarcely know why I have set out this morning to write about M.R.C.S. Those who fancy that I am about to record some startling adventure or hairbreadth escape had better accompany me no further. I have to confess that during the long, long years of our companionship, M.R.C.S. has never once done anything sensational or exciting; it has never plunged into the realm of mystery or romance; it has never plugged a hole in a leaky boat and thus saved me from a watery grave; it has never proved my identity at some tremendously critical moment; it has done nothing, in fact, to justify the eminence that my pen seems bent on giving it.

I have a friend who treats a shaggy little Australian terrier with the most touching affection, admitting it to all the privileges of a' member of the family: it once saved his youngest child from the horrid fangs of a venomous snake. I have another who wears on his watch-chain a battered coin that once saved his life under the most extraordinary circumstances. But M.R.C.S. can boast of no such valiant achievements. It has never even become well-known or famous or popular: it cannot claim to be greatly admired. Since, morning by morning, it takes up its post at the back of my neck, and is carefully concealed under the collar of my coat, it has never attracted the slightest notice or excited the most casual remark. Journalists have eyes and ears for the most trivial personal details; but, during all these years, not one of them has ever written a line about M.R.C.S. Indeed, during all these years, only two or three pairs of eyes have ever beheld it. On my dressing-table there stand a pair of candlesticks. They are adorned by a thistle with, just above it, the inscription: *A Present from Edinburgh*. As a souvenir of my visit to that noble city, many years ago, I brought them back with me. Neither of them has ever held a candle. But the candlestick on the right-hand side of the dressing-table is the home of M.R.C.S. Into the cavity intended for the candle I drop M.R.C.S. every night. In the morning it comes forth from its resting-place to begin a new day of useful but unostentatious toil. It is hidden all day and hidden all night. Nobody would miss it if, through some desolating calamity or unpardonable oversight such as I shudder to contemplate, I were never to wear it again. But the loss would fall upon me with all the poignancy of a personal bereavement.

And, when all is said and done, it is not by exciting and sensational performances that life is most enriched. It is not from the heroic or romantic people that we draw our wealthiest supplies of comfort and inspiration. The modest folk who do the commonplace things with unwavering constancy contribute incalculably to the sum total of human happiness. Romantic people are all very well in their way. It is very nice to have a few of them about. There is a young fellow walking the streets of this city who, if I gave him the opportunity, would rescue me from drowning under the most thrilling and picturesque circumstances. I have never seen him; but I feel in my bones that he is there; and it is good to know that, when I lose my balance on the bridge, his gallant services will be available. But, up to this moment, I have deprived him of the medal of the Royal Humane Society by adhering closely to the footpath and declining to fall into the water. My potential hero is a most admirable fellow, I know; yet I have to confess that, so far, the services rendered by M.R.C.S.—and by those obscure folk of whom M.R.C.S. is the natural representative— have been of immeasurably greater value to me. The world's most distinguished workers divide themselves into three classes. There are those who, like the inventor, do *extraordinary* things. There are those who, like the poet or the composer, do *ordinary* things in an *extraordinary* way. And there are those who, like M.R.C.S., do quite *ordinary* things in a quite *ordinary* way, but, because of their indomitable persistency, they do those things on a quite *extraordinary* scale.

Now this morning I caught my mind revolving a very curious question. It happens that I have a bad cold, and was compelled to spend yesterday in bed. During the day the domestic programme was carried out as usual, and, among other items, the things on the dressing-table were dusted and tidied. In the process M.R.C.S. was removed from the candlestick on the right-hand side of the table and deposited in the candlestick on the left. And this morning when, quite mechanically, I felt for M.R.C.S. in its usual place, it was not there! The sense of loss was only momentary; but it was just long enough to make me conscious of the value that I set upon my treasure. Now why, I asked myself, why have I come to attach so much sentiment to a mere collar-stud?

It is sometimes said that we value things in proportion to their cost. A mother cherishes a special affection for the child that has cost her sleepless nights and days of cruel anxiety. Jewellery is, for the most part, quite useless; its value depends upon the expenditure that it has entailed. If diamonds were sold at sixpence a quart no lover would offer and no lady would wear them. Our missionaries soon discovered that to give the Bible free of charge to the natives was to ensure its neglect. The people of India and China felt instinctively that the thing that costs nothing is worth nothing. The missionaries therefore adopted the policy of *selling* the Scriptures; and the people responded to the new order of things by buying and prizing and studying the sacred books. The principle is of wide application; but it is not of universal application. Therein lies the danger of generalizations. We are too prone to conclude that, because a certain law operates here and there, it operates everywhere. The highest function of science is to discover the exception and to modify the rule accordingly. Now, obviously, M.R.C.S. is the exception; and we must not make our laws so rigid that the production of the exception will shatter it. There are some things, and they are among life's wealthiest endowments, that come to us without the payment of any price. The air that we breathe; the water that we drink; these are things without which we could not live; yet their value in no sense depends upon their costliness.

Nor, strictly speaking, does the value that I set upon M.R.C.S. depend upon the service that it renders me. In my last paragraph I associated M.R.C.S. with the air that I breathe and the water that I drink; but there is a difference, and an important difference. For, as I said, I could not live without air, and I could not live without water; but, although it is painful to have to confess it, I could have managed very comfortably without M.R.C.S. On the day of that memorable cricket match I could have bought half-a-crown's worth of collar-studs, and, with reasonable care, the supply would have lasted my lifetime. Clearly, then, M R C.S. has not yet rendered me half-a-crown's worth of actual service; yet the offer of many half-crowns would not bring about our separation.

And, by the way, this sordid way of speaking of a sentimental subject reminds me that I owe M.R.C.S. a most abject and sincere apology. On the day of the cricket match I took it for granted that the trinket in the grass was just a common stud. I had worn it for fifteen years before I discovered that it was gold with a pearl at its base! It is an unamiable habit of ours. We take it for granted that the man to whom we are introduced is just common clay, and we treat him accordingly. Years afterwards we marvel at our blindness. He is gold, through and through!

As I ponder M.R.C.S. today, I am impressed by our amazing faculty for getting fond of things. Fond, I say, of *things*! A dog is an affectionate beast; but a dog would wear a collar for years without getting fond of it. You might change the collar some fine morning, and it would not affect old Rover in the least. We mortals are not built that way. We are compounded of sensibilities and feelings and emotions that reach out from us, like the tendrils of the ivy or the vine, and grasp anything they chance to touch. They cling sometimes to little things—like M.R.C.S.—just as the tendrils of the ivy may cling to a wisp of grass that grows from a cranny in the castle wall. But those mysterious capacities of ours were not made to cling to little things. The tendrils of the ivy were made to grasp, not the wisp that waves from the wall, but the granite of the old grey wall itself. And though my soul may sometimes cleave to trifles, the very tenacity with which it cleaves to those trifles is a reminder that it was fashioned to lay hold on things that will endure forever. Our attachment for things like M.R.C.S. is part of the infinite *within* us, and it is never completely at rest until it has taken firm hold on the infinite *beyond*.

III

THE ACCOMPANIMENT

It happened that the tram in which I was coming home last night passed the Town Hall just as the concert closed. The audience was streaming into the street, and the car quickly filled. Two young ladies, whose handsome furs only partly concealed their charming evening frocks, took seats immediately opposite me. Except by deliberately putting my fingers to my ears, how could I help listening to their conversation? I need scarcely say that I could not bring myself to behave so rudely. I therefore heard every word.

'What did you think of Yvonne Gray?' asked the girl in pale blue.

'Oh, Addie,' replied her companion, her face clouding as she spoke, 'I thought she sang divinely; but the song was simply murdered by the accompaniment.'

I heard no more. I did not wish to do so. Like a bee smothered with pollen, I felt that I had gathered as much as I could carry. I determined to unburden myself as soon as I could get to my desk this morning. And here I am! I shall have to be careful.

Music is not my forte. I recognize that I am skating on very thin ice. But, for all that, I fancy I can see my way to one or two conclusions that no expert is likely to challenge or dispute.

A song depends for its success upon a number of distinct factors. It depends partly upon the words; partly upon the enunciation and expression of those words; partly upon the music; partly upon the rendering of that music; and partly upon the capacity and mood of the hearer.

It depends to some extent upon the words. There was a time when I should have attributed to the words a paramount and supreme importance. The discipline of the years has, however, led me to modify that early judgement. It may be that I have learned to love music a little more; it may be that I have come to esteem words a little less; I do not know. I only know that, much as I like to hear the words, a song is not entirely lost upon me even though the singer's lips convey no clear syllable or concrete sentiment to my eager mind.

A few years ago I was spending a holiday at Beechington. A certain song was just then at the height of its popularity. Everybody was singing snatches of it, especially towards the close of the day. I sauntered along the sands one evening as the sun was setting, and was surprised at the number of people who were singing it, or humming it, or whistling it. It was one of those haunting airs that seemed made for the twilight, and at twilight it sprang to one's lips of its own accord.

A week or two later, in the course of a motor tour through a country district, we paused for the night at a little wayside inn. On the piano, I saw to my delight the song that I seemed to know so well. I picked it up and read the words, of which, until then, I knew only a line or two. It was a sad disillusionment. I could make nothing of them. I asked several of those present to expound to me their meaning; but they were as much in the dark as I was. Nobody could make sense of them. I then understood why I had so often heard the air crooned in the gloaming without having been able to learn the words to which it was supposed to be wedded.

Something of the same kind sometimes happens at home. In the street in which I live a very musical family resides. I enjoy sitting on the verandah of an evening listening to the distant music. I can seldom distinguish the words; but I am astonished at the degree to which my spirit is affected by the plaintiveness or the gaiety of the songs. Such experiences have taught me that the general impression created by the song depends less upon the words than I once upon a time supposed.

In the ideal state of things, however, we are not asked whether we will have bread *or* cheese, almonds *or* raisins, strawberries *or* cream. We are offered bread *and* cheese, almonds *and* raisins, strawberries *and* cream. It is not a case of the words or the music; the model singer will be careful to give us the words and the music. We all have a good deal of sympathy with Charles Finney, the eminent evangelist, who used to be extremely vexed if the words used in worship were not clearly rendered. On a very memorable occasion he rose, at the conclusion of the anthem, to lead the congregation in prayer. 'O Lord,' he exclaimed, in a voice full of genuine distress, 'we have no doubt that Thou hast known and understood all that Thy gifted servants have been singing, but, as for us, we haven't caught a blessed word!' It is a pity when, with strawberries and cream both available, we have to be satisfied with the one or with the other.

A Presbyterian minister was telling me only a few days ago of an experience that befell a missionary of his church whose duty it is to visit the lonely settlers in the vast solitudes of our Never-Never country. After riding for many miles through the virgin bush, he discerned towards evening a friendly column of smoke. Making his way towards it, he suddenly came upon a little humpy built of corrugated iron,

the home of a solitary herdsman. Delighted at seeing a human face and hearing a human voice, the man eagerly welcomed the missionary's advent and at once asked him to stay the night. Seated on boxes beside the open camp fire, the two men spent the evening in discussing a thousand themes, and each soon took the measure of the other. Among other things, the herdsman told his companion how sorely he needed rain. It had been a dry season, and, unless a change soon came, half the settlers in the district would be ruined. Strangely enough, the two had scarcely retired for the night when the heavy drops began to drum on the iron roof, and, an hour later, the roar of the rain made sleep almost impossible.

Both were astir early in the morning; and the missionary was astonished at noticing that the herdsman, as he busied himself about the preparations for breakfast, was singing, and singing a well-known hymn, and singing as one sings when all his heart is glad. The visitor was puzzled, for the singing seemed so out of keeping with the man's conversation overnight.

'I thought,' he ventured to say, 'that you did not believe in that?'

'No,' replied the man, 'I don't; *but I like the tune!*'

The incident struck me at the time as being very suggestive; and, the more I have thought of it since, the more has it grown upon me. The herdsman sang because his heart was overflowing; he sang the hymn, he said, because he liked the tune; but I cannot rid my mind of the suspicion that, the longer he sang, the less incredible and the more attractive the words themselves must have seemed to him. A man may sing 'How sweet the name of Jesus sounds' because he loves the strains of 'St. Peter'; but let him sing it long enough, and his heart will begin to acknowledge the charm of the sacred Name that his lips have so often framed.

Now this is an allegory. As the angels knew, on the night on which they proclaimed to wondering shepherds the Saviour's birth, God's message to His world is not a sermon, nor a speech, but a song. Like all songs, it consists of words set to music. The words, of course, are the words of the gospel; the words of everlasting life; the words that fell from the lips of Jesus. '*The words that I speak unto you, they are spirit and they are life.*' And these beautiful words are set to the music of beautiful lives. The Australian herdsman sang the hymn *because he loved the tune*; men listened spellbound to the words that fell from the lips of Jesus because they were set to the music of a life that was so inexpressibly lovely.

'Yvonne Gray sang divinely,' the girl opposite me said to her friend last night, 'but the song was simply murdered by the accompaniment.'

That was the tragedy of the concert at the Town Hall; and that is the tragedy of the world's history. The sweetest song that angels or men have ever heard has often been murdered by the accompaniment. Let me give one or two examples of what I mean.

Let us go West! Mr. Prescott has told us in his own vivid way how Velasquez led his conquering Spaniards, early in the sixteenth century, into Cuba. The conquest was accomplished, and the brave old warrior, Hatuey, for no other crime than the heroic resistance that he had offered to his European conquerors, was lashed to the stake and sentenced to a cruel death. As his pale-faced tormentors approached with torches to light the faggots at the hero's feet, the priests drew near and implored him to embrace the faith of the Spaniards. He declined. They multiplied their entreaties, reminding him that only by kissing the crucifix could his soul find admission into heaven.

'And will the souls of the white men go to heaven?' inquired the doomed chief.

'Most assuredly,' replied the priest. 'Then,' exclaimed Hatuey, with finely flashing eyes, 'I will not be a Christian; for I would not go to a place where I shall find men so cruel!'

The message that the priest was commissioned to carry was the message of the Cross; and there is no music in earth or heaven like it. But the accompaniment! The music was murdered by the accompaniment.

Let us go East! The gospel was introduced into Japan by Francis Xavier in 1547. The Dominicans and Franciscans who followed in the steps of that devoted pioneer were, however, men who knew nothing of his spirit and had learnt nothing from his example. Their arrogance, oppression, and cruelty made them hated by the whole population. A terrible persecution broke out in 1587, and was from time to time renewed. In 1637 there was a slaughter of thirty-seven thousand Christians, the Roman Catholic martyrs dying with the greatest possible heroism. For more than two hundred years the name of Christian was mentioned in Japan with blanched cheek and pallid lip. During that long period notice-boards stood beside the highways, ferries, and mountain-passes, bearing the following inscription:

> So long as the sun shall warm the earth, let no Christian be so bold as to come to Japan; and let all know that, be he the King of Spain himself, or the Christian's God, or the great God of all, if he violate this commandment, he shall pay for it with his head!

In the East, as in the West, the matchless music has been murdered by its accompaniment.

But I need have gone neither to the East nor to the West. The fact is that, wherever the Church has, by her influence or behaviour, misrepresented her Lord, the heavenly harmonies have been marred and men have been shocked by discords in the angel-music. The caricature of Christianity under Constantine led to the revolt against Christianity under Julian. The foul misrepresentation of

Christianity which became fashionable under Louis the Fourteenth led to the age of infidelity that reached its climax with Voltaire. Macaulay shows that the hypocrisies of a decadent Puritanism were directly responsible for the revolt against religion which disfigured the seventeenth century.

In his *Les Misérables*, Victor Hugo tells the story of the dire distress of Jean Valjean, the ex-galley slave. He was driven out of one inn and then out of another. At last he took his knapsack and stick and went away. As he strode off, some boys who had followed him from the Cross of Colbas, and seemed to have been waiting for him, threw stones at him. He turned savagely, and threatened them with his stick, and the boys dispersed like a flock of birds. He passed in front of the prison, and pulled the iron bell-handle; a wicket was opened.

'Mr. Jailer,' he said, as he humbly doffed his cap, 'would you be kind enough to open the door and give me a night's lodging!'

A voice answered, 'A prison is not an inn; get yourself arrested, and then I will open the door.'

As he did not know the streets, he wandered about without purpose. He thus reached the prefecture and then the seminary. It occurred to him that, if the influence of the Church were what it should be, the people beneath its sway would have shown more pity to an outcast like himself. At that moment he passed into Cathedral Square. The great dome towered above him. The resentment of his soul reached its climax in a striking gesture. He looked up bitterly and *shook his fist at the church*. Victor Hugo probably meant the incident to stand as an allegorical representation of the greatest tragedy in the religious experience of his country. One of the most intensely pathetic books that I have ever read is Lord Morley's *Voltaire*—the life of a sceptic by a sceptic. Again and again in the course of the volume, Lord Morley half apologizes for the iconoclasms of Voltaire. 'It cannot be too often repeated,' he says, 'that the Christianity which Voltaire assailed was not that of the Sermon on the Mount. He saw only a besotted people led in chains by a crafty priesthood; he heard only the unending repetition of records that were fictitious and of dogmas that drew a curtain of darkness over the understanding. There is no instance of Voltaire mocking at any set of men who lived good lives. He did not mock the English Quakers.' It was at the accompaniment that his soul recoiled.

If only the accompaniment last night had been in perfect tune, and in perfect time, and in perfect sympathy with the singer! I should never have seen the look of disgust on the fair face opposite me, nor heard her indignant and contemptuous words! If only the Church's accompaniment had always been in keeping with the eternal harmonies! I came upon a lovely thing the other day in Lionel Trotter's *Life of John Nicholson.* Nicholson was, of course, one of the ablest, bravest, and best of our great Indian soldiers and administrators. On one of the closing pages of Captain Trotter's biography he gives a copy of a letter written shortly after Nicholson's death which tells of the extraordinary impression made upon Nicholson's native followers by the news that he had fallen. When they heard of his gallant and glorious death, they gathered together that they might join in a united lamentation. 'What happiness can there be in living in a world which no longer holds our Nicholson?' asked one; and, suiting the action to the word, he committed suicide upon the spot.

'That,' said another, pointing to the body of his self-slain comrade, 'that is not the way to please our great chief. If we wish to see our great Nicholson again, and to look into his face without shame, we must learn to worship and serve Nicholson's God!' The rest applauded, and off they all went to the missionary's house. 'Teach us,' they implored, 'so that his God may be our God, and so that we may go to him again at last.' For a year they applied themselves with the greatest assiduity to the missionary's instructions. And, at the end of that period, their teacher being perfectly satisfied with their sincerity, and altogether delighted with their clear grasp of the Christian message, they were baptized and welcomed to the fellowship of the Church.

It was the accompaniment that did it. The missionary's message is as beautiful and wonderful as an angel's song; but it is only when it is accompanied by lives like Nicholson's that it achieves its most golden conquests.

IV

A STUDIED SLIGHT

We are living in a world of wheels; yet it is not by way of the wheels that the world's best work is done. *That* was the tremendous truth that startled and comforted the soul of Kohath in the early days of Israel's historic pilgrimage.

I

It really looked as if the sons of Kohath had been slighted—wilfully and deliberately slighted. When wealth is being distributed, somebody is invariably left out in the cold. But the omission is seldom as marked as in the case of the sons of Kohath. The task that fell to Moses seemed ridiculously simple. He had to divide six presents among the three sons of Levi. The solution appeared obvious: a little child could have shown him how to do it. But Moses had a way of his own —for reasons of his own. Instead taking the simple way, he took the sensible way. Instead of doing his work mechanically, he did it intelligently. Two and two and two make six; but, instead of giving *two* of the presents to the first of the trio, and *two* to the second, and *two* to the third, he gave *two* to the first and *none* to the second and *four* to the third. It was to the sons of Kohath that he gave *none*; and it really looked as if they had been pointedly and purposely slighted.

One of the most charming features of the Church's history and experience is the practical ingenuity that is often displayed by consecrated wealth. The princes of Israel saw Moses building the tabernacle in the wilderness. They did not pretend to understand the subtle significance of the curtains and the coverings, the rods and the pillars, the altar and the candlestick. But they saw at a glance that the entire collection would weigh several tons, and that it would be no easy matter to transport it from place to place. It occurred to them that a few wagons would be particularly useful. The world's greatest benefactors are the sagacious souls who think of such things—and see them through. And so it came to pass that, on the very day on which the tabernacle was set up, the princes of Israel presented Moses with six wagons and twelve oxen for its transportation across the wilderness.

Now the matter of the transport of the tabernacle was in the hands of the sons of Levi. And, of the sons of Levi, there were three families —the sons of Gershon, Levi's eldest son; the sons of Kohath, Levi's second son; and the sons of Merari,

Levi's youngest son. It seemed easy enough to divide six wagons and twelve oxen between three families. But Moses was too great a man to be the slave of statistics. He declined to be the tool of the obvious. Arithmetic has its place in the sun, but it is not a dominant place. There are higher laws than the laws of mathematics. Moses refused to say—as a smaller soul would have said—that *three twos are six and three fours are twelve.* And so, to the sons of Gershon, the first-born, Moses gave *two* wagons and four oxen; to the sons of Merari, the youngest, he gave *four* wagons and *eight* oxen; but '*unto the sons of Kohath he gave none.*' Who can blame the sons of Kohath for feeling that they had been slighted?

II

The multiplication of wheels has been one of the concomitants of civilization. In two or three hundred years, the number of patents granted for mechanical inventions has multiplied more than a thousandfold. From 1613 to 1763 they averaged eight per annum. From 1763 to 1852 the annual rate was two hundred and fifty. During the next eighteen years it was over two thousand. In 1877 it was three thousand two hundred. In 1914 it was nearly twelve thousand, and now it is much higher still.

The world is full of wheels; we do everything by machinery. Yet, when we are at our best, we turn our backs upon the roaring furnaces and the throbbing pistons. The most delicate tasks in the universe must all be done by hand. The typewriter, abolishing the individual impress of the old-fashioned handwritten letter, may reduce our commercial correspondence to one dead level of uniformity. But, when all is said and done, the signature cannot be typed; the signature represents the personal touch; and that personal touch is the thing that matters.

A bride was showing me her presents. There were handsome books containing the most beautifully-coloured plates. The machine that produced them must have been a perfect triumph of inventive skill. There were vases and ornaments adorned with the most exquisite patterns and chaste designs. The machinery by which they were wrought must have been simply marvellous in its ingenuity. But the climax of her fond delight was reached when she handed me a fragile and beautiful treasure that bore upon its surface a floral design of rare sweetness and delicacy.

'This,' she said proudly, 'was hand-painted!'

I remember, many years ago, being shown through a great English pottery. I saw machines so wonderful that they really seemed to think. Steel arms shot out just when their services were wanted;

they put a touch here and a tap there; and then withdrew into the invisible. I was fascinated and bewildered. But when we emerged from the vast sheds in which the main work of the pottery was being done, my guide invited me to follow him along a path that led to a small and insignificant building that stood quite apart. We left the whir of the wheels behind us, and the silence seemed strange by force of contrast. In the sheds my companion had been compelled to shout in order to make me hear; now we were speaking quietly again.

'It is here,' said my guide, pointing to the little building that we were approaching, 'it is here that our best work is done. The man to whom I am about to introduce you is the most highly-paid member of our staff.'

I was astonished and curious. In a moment, however, I entered the silent building and found an elderly gentleman, of refined and cultured bearing, dressed in white overalls, and working away with his fingers at the plastic clay before him. On the bench I saw several of his finished products. There was a fine equestrian statue—about eighteen inches high; there was a miniature replica of *The Dying Gladiator*; and there was some dainty floral work. I expressed my admiration, and he showed me photographs of masterpieces that had passed from his quiet room into some of the stateliest English homes.

'He has a marvellous touch,' exclaimed my guide as we came away. 'It is difficult enough for most of us to make a lump of clay look like a man's head; but, in five minutes, he will make a lump of clay the very image of any particular man to whom you care to introduce him. His fingers are wonderful!'

And so I learned at the pottery, as I learned in the drawing-room, that the best things are done *by hand*. Machinery has its limitations. We have music by machinery nowadays; but, however perfect the pianola may be, you miss the human touch. And who would think of clicking off a love-letter on a typewriter?

III

There is work that cannot be done by all the machinery in the world. There are burdens too precious to be committed to bullock-wagons; they must be borne by hand. *That* was why Moses gave no wagons to the sons of Kohath. They had proved themselves the most willing, the most devoted, and the most dependable of all the sons of Levi. Whenever the service of the sanctuary made some special demand, the sons of Kohath were always ready to undertake the additional task. Their unwavering constancy intensified the mystery of their great leader's neglect. It would have seemed strange if, to the son of Gershon, or to the sons of

Merari, Moses had given no wagons. But his behavior in denying a single wagon to the sons of Kohath—the most loyal and most faithful of all the Levites—seemed inexplicable. But, later on, when they discovered that they were to be entrusted with the scared vessels that no wagon could be permitted to carry, they understood. They bowed their heads, not only submissively, but gratefully. Their deprivation was the mark of their dignity. They would not have forfeited their wagonless condition if they had been offered the chariots of the sun.

Every man should aim at doing a little work by hand. We are in danger of leaving too much to the machines. We forget that there is work that cannot be done on wheels. Organization is excellent, but it has obvious limitations. Here, in the pretty little town of Clarendon, are a hundred Christian men. They band themselves together in the sacred and beautiful ties of church membership. They contribute generously to church funds, and, by so doing, pay their minister—in whose culture and fervour they take growing delight—a handsome stipend. Like the princes of Israel, who presented Moses with wagons, they like to see things done nicely and worthily and well. They love to feel, as they go the week's round, that, whilst they are pursuing the path of business and of pleasure, their minister is going in and out among the homes of Clarendon or preparing a stirring evangelistic appeal for the coming Sunday. By this excellent piece of religious organization they are each participating in a concerted endeavor to win the population of Clarendon for the kingdom of God. This is excellent, most excellent; and one feels towards these men as Moses felt towards the princes of Israel.

And yet, for all that, there is one other word to be said. Each of those hundred men has his own circle of familiar friends. In that circle he is loved and honored and revered. His word carries weight. Now no minister can hope to speak to these intimate companions of his with the authority and influence that a wise and tactful word from *him* would carry. Let him look around his home, his office, his club; and he will be surprised at the wealth of the opportunity awaiting him. The minister may do his utmost and his best; but, left to him, the winning of Clarendon will be slow and uphill work. But let each member of the church do a little work by *hand*, and there will be a throb of great spiritual prosperity throughout the lengths and breadths of the town.

It is well that our charities should be organized. There is no other way of doing good work well. Left to the caprice of individual effort, some necessitous cases would be relieved from many sources, whilst others would be overlooked and neglected. But too much must not be left to the machines. Here is

Gerald Stretford. He sends a substantial cheque every year to the Society for the Administration of Charitable Relief; and he does well. He wisely avails himself of machinery that has been established for his guidance and assistance. He knows that, sent though this channel, his munificence will be distributed systematically and with discrimination. But, if he would enjoy life's best, he must not stop at that. He must do a little handwork. Now, within half a mile of Gerald's door there is a little cottage in which old Betty Kingston lives. The poor body is quite helpless; every joint is racked with rheumatism. Betty is assisted by S.A.C.R. I suspect that it was through Gerald's good offices that the Society entered Betty's name upon its books. Its officer, in a green uniform, calls once a month with Betty's allowance, and gets her to put her cross against her name on the official receipt. The money is very welcome: I really cannot imagine what Betty would do without it; and, when Gerald catches sight of the cottage, he must feel gratified at the thought of the comfort that his generosity and influence have secured for her. But if, perhaps once a year, Gerald made it his business to look in on the old body, ask after her health, and make her feel that she was sometimes in his thought, what a red-letter day that would be for her—and for *him!* *She* would talk of nothing else for a week afterwards; and *he* would find the memory of that casual visit rushing pleasantly back upon his mind in moments of quietness and leisure. The world would be a poor place without the wheels; but there are still a few things that cannot be done by machinery. The wagons were very welcome; but there were some things that had to be carried by hand.

IV

The sons of Kohath were the most burdened and most blithe of all the descendants of Levi. The sons of Gershon led their oxen; they bore no burden and they sang no song. The sons of Merari led their oxen; they bore no burden and they sang no song. The sons of Kohath had no oxen to lead; they lifted their loads to their shoulders whenever the pilgrimage was resumed; and they sang as they bore them across the desert.

They never *saw* the vessels that they carried. The awful mysteries of the holy place were carefully wrapped up by the priests before being committed to the custody of the Levites. There are in every congregation a few simple but songful burden-bearers who know very little about the divine things with which, in the sanctuary, they deal. Others are far better informed, but they are no more devoted. Every man should make it his aim to keep his zeal up to the standard of his knowledge. There is no reason why those who know much should exhibit a smaller enthusiasm than those who know little. The sons of Kohath, with their unseen burdens, must not be allowed to put to shame the men who have gazed with open face upon those awful mysteries.

They were the most burdened and the most blithe. It is generally the way. The first woman in the world bore a baby in her arms; so will the last. The lowliest and the queenliest of women are on a level here. It is womanhood's everlasting burden and womanhood's everlasting blessing. No woman would have it otherwise.

One great day—the greatest of all great days—a man named Simon was compelled to share with Jesus the burden of the cross. He knew not what he did. Like the sons of Kohath, he carried what he did not comprehend. He only felt the galling burden of his heavy load. But, years afterwards, he understood; and, when he understood, he talked of nothing else. His load had glorified his life. The burden had become the blessing; labour had become lovesome; service had awakened song.

V

THE OLD MAN OF THE SEA

I was always very fond of Sinbad the Sailor, but I never believed in the Old Man of the Sea. We all remember the adventure. In the course of his travels, Sinbad saw, sitting by the banks of a stream, '*an old man, a comely person, who was clad from the waist downwards with a covering made of the leaves of trees.*' The old man asked Sinbad to carry him a little way. '*Accordingly*'—so runs the record—'*I advanced to him, and took him upon my shoulders, and conveyed him to the place that he had indicated to me. I then asked him to descend, but he made no attempt at doing so. He had twisted his legs round my neck; and looking at them, I saw that they were like the hide of the buffalo in blackness and roughness. So I was frightened at him, and desired to throw him from my shoulders; but I was his captive; he held me fast.*'

After long agony, Sinbad contrived to intoxicate his tormentor, and, whilst the monster lay in a drunken stupor, Sinbad slew him. Later on he met some sailors. '*Why,*' they cried, '*this man who rode upon thy shoulders is called the Old Man of the Sea, and no one ever was beneath his limbs and escaped from him excepting thee! Praise be to God for thy safety!*'

It is a very pretty story, as such stories go; but entirely unconvincing. It is not true to life. You very rarely come upon anything of the kind in actual experience. As a boy, I believed implicitly in Santa Claus, in Cinderella, in Bluebeard, and in the Man in the Moon; but when my nurse began to tell me of the Old Man of the Sea, I invariably turned sadly and sceptically away. Even a child's credulity has its limits.

In real life Sinbad would not have persisted in his struggle to hurl the monster from his back. He would first of all have grown accustomed to carrying him; he would then have fallen in love with him; and he would have ended by imploring the wretch on no account to leave him! This kind of thing happens every day. The cuckoo lays her eggs in a robin's nest. The robins are at first horrified at beholding the repulsive form of the stranger among their brood. As it grows, it pushes the young robins out of the nest and they lie dead on the grass below. But the parent-robins go on feeding and protecting the murderer of their own offspring. And why? Richard Jefferies says that there is only one possible explanation. By the time that they discover the cuckoo's true character, they have become attached to him. They have cared for him so long that they cannot bring themselves to treat him harshly. They fall in love with the tyrant and cherish him. It is the Sinbad story robed in feathers but true to fact.

In one of the finest passages of *The Mill on the Floss*, George Eliot describes the occasion on which, after the loss of the old mill, Mr. Tulliver discovers the extent of his misfortunes. He turns to honest Luke and says that he will go down and see the worst for himself. 'Aye, sir,' says Luke, 'you'll make up your mind to't a bit better when you've seen everything. You'll get used to it. That's what my mother says about her shortness of breath. She says she's made friends wi't now, though she fought agin' it sore when it first come on.' '*She's made friends wi't now!*'

It is a way we have. Like Sinbad, we often find ourselves under a troublesome necessity. We have to carry our Old Man of the Sea. But a time comes when we are relieved of the obligation. We may set the monster down if we will; but, instead of doing so, we cling to him and carry him still.

Let us return to the birds. I have spoken of the cuckoo and the robin; but look at the swallows! I am writing in Australia; autumn is well advanced; yet half a dozen swallows are flying round me whilst I scribble. They always amuse me. Time was when they had to carry their Old Man of the Sea. Inhabiting as they did the rigorous climes of Northern Europe, they were involved in the tiresome necessity of an annual migration. Those stern winters were more than the poor birds could endure. But these swallows skimming about this

Australian lawn are involved in no such obligation. The deep snows and the cruel frosts that first made the swallow a fugitive do not recur in these sunnier lands. He can drop his Old Man of the Sea if he will; the former necessity no longer presses. But he finds the ancient habit too strong to be resisted. He must still migrate, even though there be neither rhyme nor reason in his wayward flights. In the northern hemisphere, the migration is well conceived and well executed. Here it is capricious, arbitrary, and governed by no shred of principle. It is madness without method. Some of the birds summer where others winter; some simply fly a few hundred miles east or a few hundred miles west. These whimsical migrations add nothing to the safety or the comfort of the birds; they are simply an outbreak of the wanderlust; but this is an aspect of the case which they cannot pause to consider.

In the old times, and in the old climes, the migratory instinct was developed. It was developed under the stern compulsion of a dire necessity, a necessity so peremptory that it often drove the frantic mother-bird from her helpless fledglings and, at the time of the general migration, she would fly round the nest in anguish and leave them to perish miserably. Here, in the South, everything is different; yet the old habit persists in asserting its authority even though the necessity that prompted its formation has passed away. The bird might drop the burden he has borne so long, but he prefers to go on carrying it. The Old Man of the Sea is willing to descend, but Sinbad elects to carry him still.

Life is a slow process of evolution. We begin as monkeys; we develop into machines. The value of the machine depends upon the training of the monkey. At the beginning we are altogether original; towards the end we are altogether mechanical. Little children, like monkeys, are full of mischief and full of mimicry. But the things that they mimic gradually become absorbed into their own personality, and the actions that they at first perform by choice, they come at length to perform by rote. As life goes on, the monkey vanishes and the machine evolves. Life becomes regular and the old ways cannot be thrown off. How many men, for example, find it easy to retire even when they are in a position to do so? For years a man grumbles at the necessity of having every day to go to business. This is his Old Man of the Sea, and he prides himself that one day he will shake it off. He hurries away to the office in the driving rain and envies his neighbour who, having retired, is settling down to a magazine by the fire. On fine mornings he sees this selfsame neighbour sauntering round his garden smoking a pipe, and his smouldering envy flames up again. But *his* turn comes at last. He is in a position to retire! Yet, strange as it may seem, it is not an easy thing to do. He will go on for another year, and another, and another! The Old Man of the Sea is quite willing to descend, but Sinbad cannot bear to let him go!

Mark Rutherford has familiarized us with Mr. Whittaker. How Mr. Whittaker looked forward to retiring! At last the time came, but he found it more difficult than he had supposed to give up the reins and confess that the world could get on without him. But he managed it and retired. To his disgust, he found the new experience an unutterable boredom. At last, in sheer desperation, he accepted a position at a hundred a year. Oh, the wild delight of getting into the thick of things again! 'With what joy did I shut the little garden-gate and march down the road, once more somebody! I looked round, saw other little front gates open, each bystreet contributed, so that in the Kennington Road there was almost a procession moving steadily and uniformly Citywards, and *I* was in it! I was still a part of the great world; something depended on me. Fifty-six? Yes, but what was that? Many men are at their best at fifty-six!' And so Sinbad picked up the Old Man of the Sea once more and set out on his travels with a shining face!

It often happens. The back becomes so accustomed to the burden that it declines to be relieved of its load. The tasks that we once regarded as the sheerest drudgery establish such a hold upon our hearts that, when it is no longer incumbent upon us to perform them, we find it difficult to give them up. Does not the pathos of the *Tale of Two Cities* turn on this very point? Dr. Manette, in his gloomy cell in the Conciergerie—'One Hundred and Five, North Tower'—hammers away at his shoemaking until the occupation becomes so much a part of him that, long after his liberation, he relapses into it on the slightest provocation. In his "Prisoner of Chillon," Byron has something to much the same effect. Describing his release, Bonnivard says:

> And thus, when they appeared at last,
> And all my bonds aside were cast,
> These heavy walls to me had grown
> A hermitage—and all my own!
> And half I felt as they were come
> To tear me from my second home.
> With spiders I had friendship made,
> And watched them in their sullen trade.
> My very chains and I grew friends.
> So much a long communion tends
> To make us what we are: even I
> Regained my freedom with a sigh!

Here, in each instance, we have Sinbad the Sailor either clinging to his captor or lamenting his departure! 'Custom,' says Professor A. W. Momerie, 'custom is so powerful that it can even transmute pain into pleasure. Let a man perform a disagreeable action often enough, and he will by-and-by experience a sort of enjoyment in its performance. Let him live long enough in the midst of unpleasant circumstances and surroundings, and they will acquire a strange and inexplicable fascination.'

The law is inexorable. A prominent temperance worker in New Zealand once told me that it is very seldom that either a drunkard or a drunkard's wife can be persuaded to vote in favour of the closing of the licensed bars. Sinbad will not allow the Old Man of the Sea to leave him.

I have heard and read of deathbed repentances and of conversions at the eleventh hour. I do not doubt the records. But such happenings must be very rare. In a quarter of a century I have never known a man to break in death the habit of a lifetime. I have seen beautiful deaths, but they were preceded by beautiful lives. I have seen dreadful deaths, and they were preceded by dreadful lives. Men do not get out of their stride as they approach the last valley.

It is a very wonderful, a very terrible, and a very beautiful law, this strange law by which we learn to love our loads and to become fond even of our foes. It is liable to abuse, of course; but so are all the laws that ever were formed. I shall show its perils before I close, but just now I am charmed by its more amiable features. Half the tenderness of life stands related to it in some way or other. Think of the burden of motherhood! Is there a mother living who has not at some time murmured beneath the weight of her heavy, heavy load? Yet is there a mother living who has not looked wistfully and regretfully at the empty cradle and brushed a tear from her eye as her last baby has passed from under her care?

Or glance at the law in still another light. Only yesterday I had occasion to visit old Mrs. Forrester. I always enjoy a call upon her. She lives near the end of a winding avenue of silver poplars, and yesterday the trees were decked in all their autumn glory. The cottage itself is an island in an ocean of flowers. Mrs. Forrester is in the nineties; is quite helpless; and is entirely dependent on her two unmarried daughters, both of whom are well over sixty. They do everything for her and dread the dawning of a day when they will not have it to do. So does she.

'Well, Mrs. Forrester,' I said to her, in the course of our conversation yesterday, 'you've had a long spell of life; aren't you getting a little tired of it?' She looked up in surprise to see if I really meant it.

'Tired!' she exclaimed, 'oh, dear, no! I've enjoyed it too much for that, and I'm enjoying it still!'

She paused for a moment and seemed lost in thought. Then she went on, as though talking to herself.

'No, no!' she said, 'I don't want to die. How could I leave the girls? I can't bear to think of Mary and Jean left motherless!'

What did this mean? It simply meant that she had borne her maternal burden so long that it had become the habit of her mind; she could not bring herself to drop her motherly anxiety on behalf of her daughters even when it became an absurdity for her to sustain it any longer. As I walked back up the golden avenue, I thought of Mr. Tulliver, of the cuckoo in the robins' nest, of our Australian swallows, and of poor Mr. Whittaker. And I felt grateful to Mrs. Forrester for throwing a more pleasant light on the law that had made them its victims.

What with birthdays, weddings, anniversaries, and one thing and another, congratulations are fairly common in a world like this. But there are three people in the history of this planet to whom I tender congratulations of a quite uncommon kind.

I congratulate *Sinbad the Sailor* on the fact that he never made friends with the Old Man of the Sea, and gave himself no rest until the monster was slain.

I congratulate *the Prodigal Son* on the fact that he never grew accustomed to the far country, and was homesick and restless until he turned his steps once more to the father's house.

I congratulate *Bunyan's Pilgrim* on the fact that he never allowed his back to get used to the burden, but groaned beneath his load until he lost it at the Cross.

VI

BLUSHES

'Connie's blushing! That proves it!' cried Archie, clapping his hands in his pitiless glee.

He made, it will be observed, two distinct statements: the first was indisputably true; the second was as indisputably false. That poor Connie was blushing everybody could see at a glance. Whether she had begun to do so before Archie's unmannerly outburst drew all eyes upon her, I cannot say; but certainly from that moment her fair face was all aflame.

It was a public holiday; the weather conditions were perfect; we were enjoying a picnic in one of the beautiful bays on the banks of the Derwent in Tasmania. The motor-boat that had brought us was tossing at anchor near the rocks on which we had landed; the cloth was spread on the grass at the foot of a giant gum; and the conversation had taken the irresponsible turn into which it so easily drifts on such delightful occasions.

Connie was blushing; up to that point Archie was on safe, though delicate, ground. I can almost forgive him for drawing our attention to Connie's embarrassment. Blushes are very beautiful. I do not for one moment suggest that it was for that reason that Connie blushed. Blushes are not made for show. Philosophers are fond of telling us that our ordinary actions are of two kinds. There are, they say, our *voluntary* and our *involuntary* movements. There are the things that we do deliberately and of set purpose; we speak, we eat, we walk, we work. And there are the things that we do without thinking about it; our lungs, our hearts, and our digestive organs do their best work when our thoughts are over the hills and far away. Into these two classes, the philosophers assure us, our daily acts may be divided.

I respectfully suggest that there is a *third* class. There are the things that we do *voluntarily*; the things that we do *involuntarily*; and the things that we do *anti-voluntarily*. For there are some things that we cannot do if we try, yet that we do most perfectly when we struggle most frantically not to do them at all. Of all our brilliant actors and actresses, not one has ever been able to blush to order; whilst it is notorious that, the more Connie tries to dismiss her blushes, the more deeply are her cheeks suffused with crimson. I have noticed repeatedly that the harder I struggle, at the photographer's behest, to look natural, the more ridiculously unnatural I look. These, and others like them, make up the third class. They represent our *anti-voluntary* movements.

Is blushing going out of fashion? If the novels are to be believed, our great-grandmothers must have spent half their time in blushing. Here, for example, is Sir Walter Besant's *All in a Garden Fair*. I find the heroine blushing four times on a single page. 'Isabel blushed at this unexpected thrust.' 'She laughed and blushed.' 'She blushed once more.' 'Here Isabel blushed again.' Even Archie will confess that, considered as a pyrotechnic display, Connie's performance is a very tame affair compared with Isabel's. I wonder why? Blushing, as everybody knows, is a matter of nerves. For years we have been told that ours is a neurasthenic generation. Is it possible that, in this respect at any rate, we are not as decadent as we have been given to suppose? In an article entitled "The Miracle of Modern Nerves," Mr. Sidney Low declares that the most amazing revelation of the war-period was the extraordinary strength of nerve displayed on both sides. He shows that soldiers, sailors, and ordinary citizens exhibited a steadiness that had never before been approached. All the world over, men from the teeming centres of population and men from the solitudes outback vied with each other in proving that they had perfect command of themselves. So, too, did the women. The strain was simply terrific; history can produce nothing to compare with it; but the modern nerve was equal to it all.

'Connie's blushing! That proves it!' cries Archie. He is right and he is wrong. It is one thing to cry 'Fire!'; it is quite another thing to trace the cause of the conflagration. Archie is altogether right in saying that Connie is blushing; her face is all aflame. He is altogether wrong in saying that her blushes prove his accusation. Blushes never prove anything.

Readers of *Daniel Deronda* will remember that, at a critical stage in the evolution of the plot, George Eliot makes Gwendolen blush in the presence of Deronda. Her concern as to the interpretation that will be put upon her confusion only intensifies her embarrassment. But, George Eliot points out, it is never possible accurately to decipher and translate such symptoms. 'A blush,' she says, 'is no language; it is only a dubious flag-signal which may mean either of two contradictories.' Precisely; the case could not have been better stated. Connie's blushes only prove that she is in distress; as to the cause of that distress they prove nothing at all. Archie says that they prove the truth of the statement that he had previously made. They may do; or they may prove the utter falsity of that statement. The embarrassment with which we admit an imputation is so much like the embarrassment with which we resent an imputation that it is never safe to argue from the confusion to its cause.

The matter is of some practical importance. Mr. Thomas Holmes, the famous Police Court Missionary, has probably had more experience of the criminal classes than any man of our time. 'No man,' says Mr. W. Grinton Berry, 'is better known or more beloved by such people than is he.' His books are classics. I have just been reading his *Psychology and Crime*. In these pages Mr. Holmes makes a passionate but carefully reasoned appeal for a return to common sense in the treatment of crime. He is terribly afraid that the application of what is commonly called 'psychology' to criminology may do infinite harm. During the past few years an enormous number of books have been published purporting to teach the observer to analyse the criminal mind by means of external symptoms. In the nature of the case, these books have circulated principally among those who have to do with crime and criminals. Mr. Holmes regards the entire literature as pernicious and perilous in the extreme. He implores justices, jurymen, and the like utterly to ignore it. He argues that the external symptoms by which an innocent man betrays his shame at being charged with a horrible offence resemble so closely the external symptoms by which a guilty man betrays his terror and confusion that it is impossible, by any of the laws laid down in these manuals, to distinguish between them. So true is it that neither Connie's blushes, nor anybody else's, prove anything at all.

A very important case was heard in one of our principal Australian courts the other day. The accused man, who held a high and responsible position in our public life, was defended by one of our most eminent and most highly esteemed barristers. In the course of his address to the jury, this gentleman related a striking personal experience. He pointed out that the entire case against his client rested on the circumstance that, on a certain important occasion, he had been found in a situation so compromising that he had failed satisfactorily to explain it.

'But,' continued the barrister, 'it is very easy for a perfectly innocent man to place himself in a position which he can never convincingly explain. For instance,' he continued, 'I myself some years ago entered a well-known book arcade in this city. I wanted a notebook, and I particularly wanted it to be of such a size and shape that it would fit conveniently into one of my waistcoat-pockets. In an absent-minded moment I picked up a book and slipped it into the pocket to see whether it would do. I had no sooner done so than it occurred to me that I had placed myself in a most invidious position. What convincing defence could I offer if somebody suddenly tapped me on the shoulder and asked me what I meant by transferring the book from the counter to my pocket? Fortunately for me, no one saw me; and I was able to replace the book as secretly as I had taken it.'

But supposing somebody had seen! And supposing somebody had tapped this gentleman on the shoulder at that awkward moment! His confusion may be imagined. But what would his confusion prove? To a harsh observer it would prove guilt; to a kindly observer it would prove innocence; to a judicious observer it would prove nothing at all.

'That proves it!' cries Archie, with a fierce delight that only persecutors know. He is wrong. Blushes and such dubious flag-signals prove nothing at all. They may, as George Eliot says, mean either of two contradictories.

The matter has other implications. Blushes, as all speakers and preachers know to their cost, are by no means the only symptoms of nervous agitation and mental confusion. The trouble is very ancient. We have seen that Connie's great-grandmothers blushed even more profusely than does she. And, in the same way, it may comfort the speakers and preachers of the twentieth century to know that their predecessors of the sixteenth century experienced all the agonies of nervousness that they have themselves endured.

Here is a quaint old volume by Richard Bernard, vicar of Worksop, whose faithful ministry and noble life left their impress on the Pilgrim Fathers of New England. The book is entitled *The Faithfull Shepheard*, and is an appeal for earnestness and fidelity in the Christian ministry. Mr. Bernard instances some of the defects that neutralize the efforts of young ministers. They fall into unwholesome ways, he says, 'through too great feare and bashfulness which causeth hemmings, spittings, rubbing the browes, lifting up of the shoulders, nodding of the head, taking frequent hold of the cloake or gowne, fiddling with the fingers upon the breast buttons, stroaking of the beard and such-like toies.'

This is the masculine—or the ministerial—equivalent to Connie's blushes. I only mention it in order to remind Archie—and those who, like him, jump to swift conclusions—that it proves nothing. For, singularly enough, Mr. Bernard makes precisely the same remark in connexion with those ministerial embarrassments that George Eliot makes in reference to blushes. They may arise, he says, from either of two opposite causes. They seem to arise, and may do, from sheer foppishness and affectation; but Archie must not too hastily assume that they spring from such a root. They may just as easily be the outcome of over-anxiety, extreme timidity and self-distrust. The good man may be unnerved by the sense of his responsibility and the consciousness of his inability worthily to present the tremendous verities of which he speaks. I implore Archie, in this case as in Connie's, to give his unfortunate victim the benefit of the doubt. We are concocting today a

Philosophy of Confusion; and, within the compass of that philosophy, there is room for a spacious charity.

I hope to prove, before I lay down my pen, that our blushes stand for some of the highest qualities in our make-up. They furnish indisputable evidence of the esteem in which we hold each other's opinions; they bear witness to the fact that we belong to one another, that we are part and parcel of each other, that no man lives to himself and no man dies to himself. Darwin regards blushing as the most distinctively human of all the symptoms by which emotion is expressed. It is universal among men; there is no approach to it among the beasts. And he points out, most significantly, that our facial confusion invariably relates itself, not to our own thoughts about ourselves, but to the thoughts of others concerning us. Connie blushes, not because Archie's allegation is true, but because he thinks—or pretends to think—it is true. We blush, Darwin says, not because we are guilty, but because others think or know us to be guilty. 'A man reflecting on a crime committed in solitude, and stung by his conscience, does not blush; yet he will blush under the vivid recollection of a detected fault, or of one committed in the presence of others, the degree of blushing being closely related to his feeling of regard for those who have detected, witnessed, or suspected his fault.' Now this is vital; and it leads us to the crest of the hill from which we can catch our first glimpse of home.

And here, on the brow of the hill to which Darwin has brought us, we find Sir J. R. Seeley, Darwin's illustrious contemporary. And, as we confide to him the theme of our conversation, he also has something singularly suggestive to say. For, although he agrees with Darwin that conscience does not itself make a man blush, he at the same time declares that the best people in the world blush, and blush in solitude. This raises two questions. Who are the best people in the world? And why do they blush in secret? Sir John answers these questions in his *Ecce Homo*. At the height of one of his most stately and impressive arguments he claims that the superlative triumph of the gospel over all the philosophies of the schools lies in its production of the highest type of character known to men—the type that we all honour and admire and love. But then, he asks, how did the gospel achieve this triumph? The answer is simplicity itself. The gospel reveals a *Person*; and it is always under *personal* rather than under *logical* influences that men are wooed to goodness. Having won its first victory along personal lines, the gospel follows up that method. It introduces the new convert to the Church—the Church local and the Church universal—and thus links his life with all the loveliest lives that have ever been lived.

But why do these excellent people blush, and blush in secret? Again the answer is simplicity itself. The new convert forms the habit of reviewing his inmost self, not only from his own point of view, but from two other standpoints. He sees himself as he appears in the sight of that Divine Redeemer to whom the gospel has introduced him, and he sees himself as he appears in the sight of those good and gracious people with whom he has now become associated. He thinks of those—some of them living and some of them dead—from whose pure and upright lives gentleness and justice have overflowed into his own, and he asks himself, 'How would this action appear to *him*? Would she approve of it?' He is never alone. These great examples—the Authorities that he reveres—rule, not his actions only, but his inmost heart. At the recognition of some hidden defilement in his soul, he blushes in solitude, feeling all these eyes to be upon him.

So essential is it that a man should live his life in the conscious presence of a personal Saviour!

So vital is it that a man should live his life compassed about by so great a cloud of witnesses!

VII

A STORY OF CROSS PURPOSES

I have a suggestion to make. There dwell upon the face of this planet a handful of people who have exhibited a certain amount of genius in writing other men's lives. But they have none of them done as well as they might do—and for obvious reasons; they have written the lives of the wrong people. They have focused all their attention, and spent all their strength, on famous people; and, as they have themselves discovered to their cost, the lives of famous people can seldom be made interesting. The biographer is embarrassed at the start. He feels that his story is already stale. It is like telling a fairy-tale to children who have heard it a dozen times before, and who only listen so attentively to its thirteenth recital in the frantic hope that it will this time take an unexpected turn. But the biography of your celebrity can take no unexpected turn. The writer is tyrannized by truth. Moreover, he feels that his readers know his hero almost as well as he does. He is afraid to tell you how the great man looked; what he ate; what he wore; and what were his most characteristic peculiarities. These, he thinks, are familiar to everybody; and so, forsaking the personalities that are perennially interesting, he loses himself in a fog of philosophical reflection and abstract generalization.

The biographies of nonentities are invariably more fascinating. If I see in a shop window the life of a man of whom I never before heard, I always open negotiations with the bookseller on the spot. The biographer of such a man feels that he must make his hero live before you; he is careful to indulge in the most vivid and minute particulars; no item of description is considered too trivial; and thus, little by little, a living and satisfying portrait is made to appear upon the canvas. The man who writes the life of a celebrity is paralysed by his hero's fame; the man who writes the life of a nonentity has all the secrets up his sleeve. The stars in their courses are fighting in his favour.

But my suggestion! Let one of our really brilliant biographers put on his hat tomorrow morning; let him step out into the street; let him stop, as politely as possible, the first person that he happens to meet; and let him break to that astonished individual the sensational news that he is about to write his—or her—biography. It does not matter in the least who the person is. It may be a millionaire or it may be an organ-grinder; or, for that matter, it may be the millionaire's mastiff or the organ-grinder's monkey. Jack London has written a masterly biography of a wolf; the mastiff and the monkey ought not, therefore, to prove impossible.

But, leaving wolves and mastiffs and monkeys out of our reckoning, I am convinced that a book, written by a skilful hand, on the lines I have suggested, would prove of really absorbing interest. There is no drama like the drama of reality. The man whose biography was not worth writing has never yet been born. Let it but be written with candour, with simplicity, with honesty—the struggle tellingly recorded and the secret soul laid bare—and any such volume would hold the reader spellbound from the first page to the last.

And, after all, every life has its purple patches, its hours of wild romance, its golden dreams, its heartbreak and its bloodshed. I often think of Mosgiel—the little Scottish settlement in New Zealand in which I spent the first twelve years of my ministerial life. In describing a secluded English hamlet, fifty miles from London, Mark Rutherford says that 'it might be supposed that there was no romance in the little village of Cowfold. There could not be a greater mistake. The Garden of Eden; the murder of Cain; the Deluge; the salvation of Noah; the exodus from Egypt; David and Bathsheba, with the murder of Uriah; the Assyrian invasion; the Incarnation; the Atonement and the Resurrection from the Dead—all these happened in Cowfold, and were, perhaps, more interesting there because they could be studied in detail, and the records were authentic.'

I know that this was true of Mosgiel. I was led to these reflections by consulting my birthday book. Against today's date I find the name of Gilbert Thomas. And I can never recall the familiar face of Gilbert Thomas without recalling also a set of circumstances that, if embodied in a novel, would be scouted as wildly improbable. Yet this narrative will be read by many who are intimate with all the facts. And, in all human probability, stranger things happen every day and perish forgotten for want of a chronicler.

I was sitting, one sunny October morning, on the broad verandah of my Mosgiel manse. The mountains hemmed me in on every side. October, in these latitudes, is the loveliest month of the whole year. The first delicious breath of summer is in the air; the gardens are aglow with spring flowers; the bush around is waking up; and on every bough the birds are busy. Far across the plain before me, the farmers were hard at work in anticipation of a wealthy season. I was just becoming absorbed in my book when the gate swung open and Gilbert Thomas came down the gravel path. He was a Sunday-school teacher, and held several offices of responsibility in connexion with the church. After commenting on the beauty of the morning and the promise of the fields, he told me that he was in a good deal of perplexity, and asked if I had time to listen to his story. I brought out a second arm-chair and bade him proceed. And this is what he told me.

'I was born in England,' he began, 'and was one of a large family. I was the first to leave the old home. I married and came out to New Zealand. But, as the years went on, one member of the family after another followed my example. One went to South Africa, one to Canada, one to Western Australia, until at last the old folks were left by themselves. Then I received the news that my father had died, and my mother remained alone. The brother who had settled in South Africa urged her to leave England and make her home with him. He was doing well and had plenty of room for her. At length she consented, and sailed for Cape Town. After a year or two, my brother contracted a fever and suddenly died. I have never heard of my mother since. That was years ago. I have tried in every possible way to trace her; but in vain. And now I am beginning to feel that it is my duty to go to South Africa and search for her. What do you think?'

I allowed the bees in the garden and the birds in the hedge-row to have things to themselves for a few minutes whilst I sat in silence. I found it difficult to advise him. I reminded him at last that he was not a wealthy man, that he had a wife and young children dependent upon his labour, and that their claim must be considered. I produced an atlas, and pointed out that South Africa is an enormous territory, and that the chances of finding an obscure individual there were, to say the least of it, remote. I said, too, that the recent war—the Boer war of 1900—had brought about a condition of general unsettlement and dislocation which would make his difficult task still more baffling. And I suggested that it was extremely probable, especially in view of her silence, that his mother was either dead or had married again, and that, in the latter case, her new and unknown name might prove a fatal obstacle to his search. I emphasized all these points, not without considerable reluctance. It seemed ill to become a Christian minister to dissuade a man from so laudable a pilgrimage as that which he proposed. A mother is a mother. And so I made it clear that whilst I had felt it right to lay before him the stupendous difficulties that confronted him, I was by no means certain that he ought not to go. I urged him to make quite sure that he had exhausted all other means of discovering his mother's where-abouts; to satisfy himself that he could afford, whilst prosecuting his great search, to provide for his wife and children; and then to see me again.

He thanked me and left. A few months later, when the plain was golden with harvest and the first suspicion of frost was in the air, he came again. He had established fresh communications and made more exhaustive inquiries; but all had proved fruitless. He felt that he could never rest so long as his mother's fate, or her happiness, were uncertain. He had the previous evening discussed the matter for the last time with his wife, and they had agreed that it was best that he should go. There was, therefore, nothing further to be said.

We held a social at the church to bid him farewell, and a modest presentation was made. The next day he was to leave. Mosgiel is about ten miles from Dunedin, the port of his departure, and a number of us resolved to accompany him to the ship. The *Mararoa* put to sea at about four o'clock in the afternoon. As the huge liner glided majestically down the channel, we stood on the wharf—his wife and children, with some thirty or forty friends—and waved to him until his handkerchief was no longer discernible. Then, with that sensation of depression which is peculiar to the departure of the 'outward bound,' we sadly and silently retraced our steps to the station. It was almost dusk when we left the train at Mosgiel and walked in a straggling procession along the station road towards our several homes. We had not gone far when I noticed an elderly lady, clothed in black, a stranger in the district, evidently embarrassed and perplexed. I approached her, and asked if I could be of any assistance.

'Do you know where Gilbert Thomas lives?' she asked.

'I know his home, but I am afraid you will not find him there.'

'You don't mean that he's dead?' she inquired anxiously.

'No indeed,' I answered, ashamed of the ambiguity of my former reply, 'but he has left this very afternoon on a long voyage, and, as a matter of fact, my friends and I have just been to see him off.'

'A long voyage!' she almost screamed; 'a long voyage! Why, wherever has he gone?'

'He has sailed for South Africa to search for his mother,' I explained to her; 'he has not heard from her for many years.'

She became deadly pale and seized my hand. 'Gone to South Africa to search for his mother!' she cried. 'Why, *I am his mother!* I have arrived this very day from South Africa to look for him!'

It would still have been possible, had we climbed the hill, to have seen the great ship passing down the coast. But it would have been a tantalizing experience and nothing would have been gained. By this time the wife of the unhappy voyager had joined us, and had grasped the extraordinary development of the situation. We went together to the post office to send cablegrams to ports of call, in hope of intercepting him. Wireless was then unknown. And then they went home together in the twilight, the lonely wife and the long-lost mother; to comfort each other as best they could until the wanderer's return.

How did it all end? How *should* it all end? The trouble about the present method of writing biographies is that they are bound to end well. The biographers only write about successful men. One of the beauties of my suggestion is that the man whom the biographer happens to meet as he steps out on to the public thoroughfare may be a failure —a deadbeat, a gaol-bird or a tramp. In that case the volume will be all the more exciting. We badly need a few biographies with bad endings. Our libraries—public and private—are woefully short in that department of literature. And it is a very interesting and very profitable department. Failures are tragically instructive.

This story of mine ends badly. Gilbert Thomas and his mother were disappointed in each other. Neither of them had made allowance for the years, and the changes that come with the years. They had grown away from each other. *She* had lived a rough, discordant life in an up-country mining town in the Transvaal; she had acquired a taste for drink and for pleasures of the coarser kind. *He,* on the other hand, had come under gentler and more gracious influences, had joined the Church, and had taken an active and honourable part in several Christian enterprises. Poor Gilbert! For six months he struggled bravely with his sorrow and did his utmost to reconcile his mother to the atmosphere of his home. But it was useless. She announced her intention of returning to South Africa; and, not long after, he found himself standing where we had stood before, waving to the ship that bore his mother from him. He never saw or heard of her again.

I suppose that my story shows, if it shows anything, that the dearest and sweetest relationships of life have one peculiarity in common with the most ordinary things. They go to pieces unless kept in constant repair. Neglect spells destruction. I am apt to think that, whilst *I* change and grow, the rest of the world stands still; *I* may alter but everybody else remains the same. We forget that the friend from whom we parted years and years ago has, like ourselves, grown older. There is but One upon whose eternal youth the treacherous years make no impression; there is but One with whose likeness, when we awake after the dream of Time, we shall be perfectly satisfied. And, unless we keep that friendship in repair, we may even find that as the years have run their sluggish course, we have drifted away from *Him*.

PART III

I

ON PICKING PEOPLE'S BRAINS

I have no idea what they were talking about. We were staying at a commodious old boarding-house up among the mountains. It was a perfect morning, and the boarders were, with scarcely an exception, awaiting on the verandah the ringing of the breakfast-bell. I was seated near the door holding a book in my hand, but devoting all my attention to the rugged and snow-capped heights around me and the blue lake spread out at my feet. Two gentlemen, bareheaded, were promenading the verandah side by side. As they passed and repassed me, I caught snippets of their conversation; but it did not arrest me until one of them suddenly and emphatically exclaimed, with the air of a man who settles the question for all time—and all eternity:

'Well, there may be a difference; but, if so, I can't see it. It seems to me that the man who picks your brains is as bad as the man who picks your pocket!'

The breakfast-bell drowned their voices and prevented further discussion. Perhaps the conversation was never resumed. One does not like to think that it perished at such a promising stage in its career, the breakfast-bell tolling its funeral knell. I therefore resume it today. And I resume it by assuring the gentleman who uttered his dictum with such confidence that he has not spoken the last word on the subject.

There is an essential and elemental and ethical difference between picking a man's brains and picking his pockets. The difference can be stated in a word. Brains, like peaches, were made to be picked. Pockets weren't.

It is five and twenty years, almost to the day, since I sat on that verandah at Lake Wakatipu and overheard the observation that I am challenging today. I should have challenged it before, perhaps even at the time, but I saw no chance of reaching finality. It would have been a case of my opinion against his. *He* would have clung to his dictum about the pockets, and *I* should have stated my dictum about the peaches, and we should have reached no clear conclusion. I had no witnesses. But today I am more fortunate. I have been reading Sir Arthur Quiller-Couch's *Memoir of Arthur John Butler*, the eminent Dante scholar. Among the best things in the book are Butler's letters. One of them is to his son, who has just left Eton and gone to Cambridge. He urges him, as is natural in the circumstances, to make the most of his opportunities. And then he holds himself up to his boy, not as an example, but as a warning. 'Look at me,' he says. 'I held good cards; I did not play them as I ought to have done; and I am where I am. Now I have to toil at hackwork, at a time of life when most people are beginning to take in their sails.'

This is all very abstract and general; has he nothing to say that is definite and particular? He has. 'You should practise,' he says, 'the operation known as *picking people's brains*. In nine cases out of ten they like it. As for your coach and your lecturers, it is what they are there for. Let nothing stand between you and your purpose. Suppose—to take a perfectly imaginary case—suppose there is some bit of knowledge essential to your work which you can only get by writing to the Emperor of China, you should write to the Emperor of China and get a Chinese scholar to translate it for you.'

If only I could have had Butler with me on the New Zealand verandah that morning! The scenery would have been altogether to his taste, for he was not only a great scholar, but a clever mountaineer. If only I could have had a copy of his letter to his son! But it had not then been published! But here it is, lying before me now, and it is the sudden discovery of this unexpected treasure that has sent my mind flying back across the years.

I wonder what became of my fellow boarder! I have never seen or heard of him since. We were mere 'ships that pass in the night.' I wonder if he has chanced upon the *Memoir of Butler*? But it does not matter. For what I have learned through perusing these interesting pages, my fellow boarder will have learned in some other way. As life goes on, it teaches us all, in one way or another, the folly of picking people's pockets and the wisdom of picking people's brains.

Every man of fifty has two bitter regrets. He realizes that he has committed in his time two unpardonable sins. He is haunted by the memory of the questions that he failed to *answer*, and he is tortured by the memory of the questions that he failed to ask. On his fiftieth birthday a man looks back with shame and contrition on the occasions when others have desired to pick his brains and he has churlishly resented the operation; and he looks back with sadness on the opportunities, that he missed of picking the brains of other people. As he muses pensively on the *first* of these regrets, there rush to his mind the faces of all the little children whose questions he treated with impatience; as he reflects upon the *second*, his fancy conjures up the faces of the old folk whom he can question no more.

In *Oliver Twist*, Dickens has described the children who are clever at picking pockets; but in *Dombey and Son* he has described the child who is clever at picking brains. Poor little Paul Dombey! Dickens used to say that the day on which he wrote the account of Paul's death was one of the saddest and most tearful days of his life; and we can readily understand it. Anybody who caught a glimpse of little Paul could see that he was not long for this world; and it seemed as though he was determined, during his brief stay, to gather as much wisdom as possible. He picked everybody's brains. He was forever asking questions. He asked questions that neither his sister nor his nurse nor his father could answer. And when, later on, for the sake of the sea-air, he was sent to the establishment of the immaculate Mrs. Pipchin, at Brighton, he plied her with his questions, too. That, as Butler would say, is what she was there for; but she did not relish the operation for all that. She spent her days in fearful apprehension as to what he was going to ask next. She felt it an unspeakable humiliation to spend half her time confessing her ignorance: so one day, in sheer desperation, she reminded her pale-faced little pupil of the boy who, she said, was gored to death by a mad bull for asking questions. But this alarming recital only involved her in further inquiries. How, Paul asked, did the bull know that the boy was in the habit of asking questions—especially if the bull was mad? Paul was an incorrigible brain-picker!

'What's money, father?' he asked of the great financier. 'Is it a good thing or a bad thing? If it is a bad thing, why are you so fond of it? And, if it is a good thing, why didn't it save my mamma? Why did mamma have to die?'

And then, listening to the murmur of the sea, he asked his famous question about its restless waters. 'What is it,' he asked, 'that the waves are always saying?'

Paul Dombey represents—as his creator probably designed him to do—all that is best in childhood. Children are sent into the world to pick our brains, and they learn the art with even greater facility than the children in Fagin's thieves' kitchen learned to pick pockets. Alfred Russel Wallace said of Darwin that his whole character was reflected in the restless inquisitiveness of his boyhood. He demanded to know the '*how?*' and the '*why?*' and the '*what for?*' of everything; and he maintained his insatiable curiosity unabated to the end. It would have been one of the tragedies of civilization—a tragedy that would have been none the less calamitous because, in the nature of the case, it would have been unsuspected and unrecorded—if unsympathetic parents or unimaginative teachers had cured young Darwin of his penchant for interrogation. Had he fallen into the clutches of Mrs. Pipchin she would certainly have threatened him with a dreadful death on the horns of an angry bull, and, if she had succeeded in silencing him by that ruse, she would have done more damage than all the mad bulls since the world began.

In his *Wood Magic*, Richard Jefferies points out, in his inimitable way, that it is part of the grandeur of man that he has it in him to ask questions. He is essentially a brain-picker. Sir Bevis asks the grasshopper why he doesn't hop straight. '*Why?*' repeats the grasshopper, '*why? why? why?* I never heard anything say "*why?*" before! There is always a great deal of talking going on, for the trees have nothing else to do but to gossip with each other; but they never ask *why? why? why?* Even the beasts and the birds take things pretty much for granted. They stare at the marvels about them, but display little or no curiosity. It is the glory of childhood, on the contrary, that it is endowed with an infinite capacity for wonder.

> I asked my papa why the world
>   Is round instead of square,
> And why the piggies' tails are curled,
>   And why fish don't breathe air,
> And why the moon don't hit a star,
>   And why the dark is black,
> And jest how many birds there are,
>   And will the wind come back?
> And why a horse can't learn to moo,
>   And why a cow can't neigh,
> And do the fairies live on dew?
>   And what makes hair grow grey?
> And why the grass is always green,
>   Instead of sometimes blue,
> And why a bean will grow a bean,
>   And not an apple, too.

It is a pity that nobody could answer Paul Dombey's questions; it is a thousand pities that nobody seriously tried. Paul soon drooped and died.

And, when they talked about him afterwards, his sister and his nurse and his teacher and his father must often have felt sorry that they had not wrestled more patiently with the queer questions that he was always propounding.

The conscience of every man of fifty presents him at times with the image of a roguish little face whose first brave ventures in the art of brain-picking were rendered fruitless by his own irritability and impatience. 'Oh, do be quiet!' he said, or, worse still, 'Run away and ask mother!' And now, at fifty, he thinks of what might have been. That roguish face is little no longer; it is set on a pair of stalwart shoulders; and is lifted, by a tall athletic frame, six feet from the ground. And the pity of it is that, with the years, father and son have drifted apart. And the father knows that the son is not altogether to blame. There was a time when the boy wanted to learn and the father was unwilling to teach; *now* the father wants to teach but the son is unwilling to learn. Life is full of such retributions. At fifty, a man remembers that, long ago, in the temple, a boyish face looked up into the faces of the doctors, 'both hearing them and asking them questions.' After all, his boy was only doing what *that* boy did!

I tapped a deep and unsuspected vein of pathos in the course of my visitation the other afternoon. I was struck by the beauty of a photograph upon the wall. It was the portrait of a child, and in the face there was extraordinary depth and sweetness. I stepped towards it to examine it more closely; and I saw at once that my action had awakened the very tenderest memories.

'Yes,' said my hostess, 'that was our Claude: I wish you could have known him. He was such a robust, sturdy little fellow; and, when he was taken ill, we never dreamed that the worst might happen. He lay in his own bedroom just off the living-room. As he grew rapidly worse, I became worried and, perhaps, a little irritable. He kept calling me and asking me questions. Such queer questions they were. I didn't know how to answer him, and I was too upset to try. At last I took him a bright new penny that the grocer had just given me among the change. "Here, Claude," I said, "I'll give you a penny to be quite quiet, and to ask no more questions!" He smiled—a sad little smile—and seemed pleased. And next morning,' she added, after a struggle with her emotion, 'next morning, when we took his hands to fold them on his breast, the penny was firmly clasped in one of them. I can never forgive myself. How many pennies would I give now just to hear him ask one question more!'

There, then, viewed first from the *masculine* and then from the *feminine* point of view, is the first of the regrets that come to us at fifty. And the second? Concerning the *second*, the *Poet at the Breakfast Table* has something to say. In one of his intimate and confidential outbursts, he declares that, among the regrets that mingle with our graver sorrows for the old friends whom we have lost, are our omissions to ask them many questions that they could so easily have answered and would have been so pleased to have been asked. The Poet evidently felt the matter somewhat poignantly, for, before closing the book, he heaves another sigh over the same futile but pathetic reflection. He is speaking of the old folk about him. 'If,' he exclaims, 'if we did but know how to question these charming old people before it is too late! About ten years, more or less, after the generation in advance of our own has all died off, it occurs to us all at once. "There! I can ask my old friend what he knows of that picture: it must be a Copley: or of that house and its legends, about which there is such a mystery. He will know all about it!" But too late! Too late!'

Too late to have our brains picked by those who were sent into the world to pick them!

Too late to pick the brains that we ourselves were sent into the world to pick!

In his lonely hut on the banks of the Merrimac Richard Groome lay ill. His daughter was his only companion, and he was bidding her to leave him.

'All that I need for my body is within my reach,' he said, 'but there are things without which I dare not die. I have heard that there hath arrived of late a godly and zealous man, one Roger Williams, who is being sorely harassed for his faith. Hasten to him, my daughter, and seek of him the knowledge without which neither my head nor heart can rest. Ask him the questions that I bid thee.'

Margaret took pencil and paper and bade him proceed.

'Ask him if, like me, he lay for many years under the conviction of guilt. Ask him if, like me, he obstinately rejected the messages of grace and darkened the illumination that visited him. Ask him by what means one whose heart hath been as hard as mine may obtain favour in the sight of heaven; ask him———'

But I need not give the whole list which Margaret took down at his dictation. There are thirty-seven questions, all great ones. Richard Groome, on his deathbed, was practising the art of brain-picking on a noble scale. He was guided by a true instinct. He vaguely felt that every man's experience is a treasure which he holds in trust for others. Brains and hearts, like pears and peaches, are made to be picked. As she hurried through those vast forests of maple and chestnut and cedar and pine, Margaret Groome felt as a man feels who bears dispatches upon which the fate of an army depends. And, when, a little later, she retraced her steps bearing the message that brought peace and comfort to her father's burdened mind and fleeting spirit, she seemed to herself to be like a golden argosy, full-freighted.

II

A NERVOUS BREAKDOWN

I

Nerves are nasty things to argue with. They never play the game. The facts on which they base their contentions are totally unreliable; and the conclusions that they erect upon that treacherous foundation are—as you discover afterwards—preposterous and grotesque. The pity is that you do not notice the absurdity of those deductions at the time. At the time, you accept all their statements at face value, and you listen to their doleful inferences with as much respect as if you were bowed in the presence of an oracle.

I remember the dance that they led poor John Broadbanks just before his long illness. He had experienced a trying winter, and was, as his subsequent collapse proved, only too clearly, very much run down. His face, as he arrived at the manse one Monday morning, was painfully haggard and drawn. He laughed bravely as we shook hands, and insisted on setting out at once on our usual stroll across the fields; but I could see that he was not well. Seated on the crest of a small hillock a few minutes afterwards, I asked if he felt tired.

'I've had a horrid night,' he explained. 'I suppose it was a reaction after the work of yesterday. I had glorious services, especially in the evening. I think my sermon last night was the best I've preached at Silverstream yet; but in the course of its delivery I made two ridiculous mistakes. I misquoted a passage and mispronounced a word. I ought, of course, to have known better. I thought I knew the passage perfectly, and did not trouble to rehearse it; and, as for the word, I never intended to use it. It came to me on the spur of the moment, and I had blurted it out before the question of its exact pronunciation occurred to me. Neither blunder mattered much, and it is very possible that neither was noticed. But, as soon as I laid my head upon my pillow, both these wretched things were up and at me. When I first discovered the mistakes that I had made, they looked to me like two small pimples on a very pretty face. But, as I tossed to and fro in the darkness, the pimples grew and grew until there was no face left. It seemed to me that the impression created by those two hideous blunders had more than obliterated the good effects produced by the services of the day. I saw all the young people of the congregation giggling at my stupidity. I fancied I saw their parents rebuking the levity of their sons and daughters, and saying all that they could say in palliation of my ignorance. But I could see that, in their hearts, these good people pitied me and wished that they had as their minister a man who could command their children's respect. My brain was on fire. I tossed about for hours. I felt that I could never enter the pulpit and face those same people again. I see this morning the absurdity of my distress; but, as you probably know as well as I do, *you can't argue with your nerves in the night.*'

Precisely! You lie still and listen to them! They make the wildest statements and you believe them! They draw the most alarming deductions and you accept them! They know that you are too tired to fight, and they take a base advantage of your weariness. They shout and scream and scold, and you yield your lacerated soul to their mercy. In the morning you look back with contempt upon your own pusillanimity. You thirst for revenge. But it is too late. Your tormentors have slunk off to their lairs to wait another chance.

The smoke of the train, as it rose from among the hills, reminded us that lunch-time was approaching. We walked back to the manse another way. It was the last time, for more than six months, that we had John Broadbanks as our guest. I was often at Silverstream during his long illness; and then when he could move about, the doctors sent him away for three months' fishing and shooting among the great New Zealand lakes and mountains.

It was a red-letter day with us all when he came back strong and well.

II

The greatest story on record of a nervous breakdown occurs in the Old Testament. The strain that led up to Elijah's collapse must have been terrific. For more than three years the sole responsibility of a great national crisis rested upon his shoulders. Every man's hand was against him, and the king had put a price upon his head. For months and months he moved in the midst of miracles. Life was intense beyond conception. Then came the dramatic ordeal of Mount Carmel; the renunciation by the people of their foreign gods; the destruction of the priests; the breaking of the drought; the savage threat of Jezebel; and—the pitiful collapse!

'He arose and fled for his life, and he went a day's journey into the wilderness, and came and sat down under a juniper-tree, and requested for himself that he might die!'

The minister whose nerves fly at him like furies as soon as they get him into the darkness on Sunday night will understand the incident perfectly. There may be passages in his Bible on which he will have need of expositors and commentaries. He will need no expositors and commentaries on this.

It is the last straw that breaks the camel's back. Every climber knows what it is, on reaching the crag that he had supposed to be the summit, to see another height still to be scaled. Every traveller knows what it is, on reaching the point that he took to be the end of the road, to see another long stretch unwinding itself before him. Every mother knows what it is, on coming to the task that she mistook for the last of the day, to find yet another pile of garments that must be mended before bed-time. Elijah had imagined that Carmel had settled everything. The people had acclaimed Jehovah as the true God; the alien priests were dead; the king had returned to his palace convinced and satisfied. Elijah was relieved at having reached the end of the long and exhausting struggle. But now a new factor entered into the situation. The queen's threat showed that the battle was not yet won. There comes a time when a man feels that he has reached the limits of endurance; he has stood as much as he can stand; '*then Elijah arose and fled for his life!*'

III

The pity of it is that it might have been prevented —and should have been prevented. Elijah was driven to despair, not by his foes, but by his friends. If only those who admired and honoured and loved him had told him so, the disaster could never have happened. He thought—and had reason to think—that he was standing alone against the world, the flesh, and the devil. He thought—and had reason to think—that he was wrestling single-handed against principalities and powers, against the rulers of the darkness of this world, against spiritual wickedness in high places. He learned when it was too late that he had seven thousand secret sympathizers!

Many a prophet and many a minister has had to tread that dark and lonely road. Indeed, the great Lord of all the prophets and of all the ministers was called upon to tread it. He lived His lonely life and wrought His wondrous works; but nothing seemed to come of it; and at last they crucified Him. It was only afterwards, on the day of Pentecost, that the result of His ministry began to appear.

Francesca Alexander has a poem in which she tells of a hermit who dwelt in a cave among the mountains. He fasted and prayed, and endeavoured by every means in his power to purge his soul of all evil and adorn it with spiritual beauty. He fancied that he alone cared about such things; and as, from his cave, he sometimes saw at night the twinkling lights of the cottages about the pineclad valleys, he wept that the people dwelling in them had no love for higher things. One day, however, he was commanded to set out on a journey among the towns and hamlets round about him. All sorts of unlikely people were moved to open their hearts to him. He was astonished at the world's wealth of hidden goodness. He returned to his cave, and, of an evening, found a new delight in contemplating the valley that lay below. He thought, as he

> . . . saw the twinkling star-like glow
> Of light, in the cottage windows far—
> How many God's hidden servants are!

When a minister is depressed by the dearth of conversions, he should indulge in a little arithmetic. He should carefully count his converts and put down the number on a sheet of paper. He should then read the story of Jesus, culminating in the record of the day of Pentecost. He should then multiply the figure on the sheet of paper by three thousand, and it will not be far out. Or, if this does not produce the desired effect, let him read the story of Elijah. He will then multiply the number on his sheet of paper by seven thousand. The secretaries who compile the ecclesiastical returns, and the statisticians who tabulate the official figures, may shake their heads and decline to admit the result of these computations among their elaborate and carefully-prepared returns; but never mind! They strain out the gnat and swallow the camel. The figures that they reject are at least as accurate as many that they embalm and immortalize. If the Old and the New Testaments mean anything, they mean that my suggestion is perfectly sound.

There is such a thing as the Church outside the Churches, the Church that is three thousand or seven thousand times as strong, in point of numbers, as the Church *within* the Churches. There ought, of course, to be no such Church. If, in Elijah's day, the Church outside the Churches had displayed the courage of its convictions, the prophet's faith might have been saved from shipwreck. He could never, then, have lifted to heaven that bitter cry '*I, even I only, am left!*' And if, in a later day, the Church outside the Churches had declared itself, the darkest chapters in the New Testament would have been differently written.

IV

It was, I repeat, a *nervous* rather than a *spiritual* breakdown. The result proves that. Like the prodigal, Elijah fled to the far country; but heaven treated him, not as a prodigal, but as a patient. Is there any passage in the Old Testament more tender or more touching than the story of the radiant experience that came to Elijah under the juniper-tree? Every minister who is tired out or run down; every minister who is threatened with, or has been overtaken by, a nervous breakdown, should read it every morning and every evening till all is well again. When a man's nerve is shattered, and he has come to the end of everything, he needs gentle and restful companionship. Heaven sent an angel! And the angel brought no rebuke, no word of censure, no stern imperative command to return. He brought nourishing food to strengthen the prophet's exhausted frame; drink to revive and exhilarate him; a glowing fire to cheer and comfort his loneliness; and the boon of sleep to soothe and renew his overtaxed powers. And then, when the angel had twice presided over the administration of those heavenly hospitalities, he ordered the prophet away into the solitudes for prolonged rest and quiet.

The whole idyll is intensely beautiful. I dealt with it in church the other Sunday. And, in order that the congregation might catch the pathos of it all, I read the four verses about the angel with the cake and the cruse, and then read four verses from Mr. C. J. Dennis' "Sentimental Bloke." I refer, of course, to the verses that deal with poor Bill's collapse and recovery. It happened soon after his wedding. Doreen was his very own at last, and their home was as happy as the home of their dreams. But, one fatal night, Bill met some old companions; they fell to drinking and then to gambling and then to more drinking; and at last Bill turned his steps homeward in the early hours of the morning in a condition in which he was ashamed to present himself to Doreen. But, he says,

> She never magged; she never said no word;
> But sat an' looked at me an' never stirred.

I could a' bluffed it out if she 'ad been
Fair narked, an' let me 'ave it wiv 'er tongue;
But silence told me 'ow 'er 'eart wus wrung,
    Poor 'urt Doreen!
Gorstruth! I'd sooner fight wiv fifty men
Than git one look like that frum 'er agen!

An' then, I sneaks to bed, an' feels dead crook,
Fer golden quids I couldn't face that look—
    That trouble in the eyes uv my Doreen.
Aw, strike! Wot made me go an' do this thing?
I feel jist like a chewed-up bit of string,
    An' rotten mean!
Fer 'arf an hour I lies there feelin' cheap;
An' then I s'pose I muster fell asleep.

' 'Ere, kid, drink this!' . . . I wakes an' lifts me 'ead,
An' sees 'er standin' there beside the bed;
    A basin in 'er 'ands; an' in 'er eyes—
(Eyes that wiv unshed tears is shinin' wet)—
The sorter look I never shall ferget,
    Until I dies.
' 'Ere, kid, drink this,' she sez, an' smiles at me.
I looks, an' spare me days! *It wus beef-tea!*

Beef-tea! She treats me like a hinvaleed!
Me! that 'ad caused 'er lovin' 'eart to bleed.
    It 'urt me worse than maggin' fer a week!
'Er I 'oo 'ad right to turn dead sour on me,
Fergives like that, an' feeds me wif beef-tea. . . .
    I tries to speak;
An' then—I ain't ashamed o' wot I did—
I 'ides me face . . . an' blubbers like a kid.

'She treats me like a hinvaleed!' exclaimed Bill in
surprise. That is exactly how Heaven treated the
prodigal prophet. 'I am treated as an invalid!' said
Elijah to himself, as he looked upon the cake and

the cruse and the glowing coals. There is a special place in the divine sympathy for the man whose nerve has failed him.

'*Doreen fergives like that, an' feeds me wif beef-tea!*' It was some such thought that won Elijah back to his old consecration and his old service. The mercy of God will follow a spent man anywhere and forgive him anything!

III

BLACK SHEEP

I have just returned from a long and delightful tour through one of the wealthiest pastoral districts of Australia. I saw sheep everywhere. And, as though to vindicate the ancient gibe, I noticed a black sheep in nearly every flock. But what of that? The black sheep is no worse than other sheep. He is no more stupid, no more obstinate, no more vicious than his white companions. He gives as much wool and he makes as good mutton.

Indeed, one large sheep-owner assured me that he is always pleased when he finds himself possessed of enough black sheep to enable him to make up a bale of black wool; he can get better prices for black wool than for white wool; the blackness is fast; it will not wash out. Another farmer told me of his futile attempts to breed black sheep. He described, too, the disgust that he felt when, after a generation or two of apparent success, he found his inky sheep producing lambs of almost snowy whiteness!

No, no; black sheep are not *bad* sheep; they are merely *exceptional* sheep; and between the *exceptional* and the *vicious* there is all the difference in the world.

It is high time that we came to some sort of understanding on this subject. There is scarcely a theme under the sun on which we talk so much nonsense. The statement that 'the exception proves the rule' is the last refuge of a beaten controversialist; and it is a miserably inadequate refuge. How can the exception prove the rule? The black sheep does not prove that all sheep are white; it proves the very reverse; it proves that all sheep are *not* white. The exception, so far from proving the rule, explodes the rule; shatters it to fragments; leaves it without a leg to stand upon.

The millennium will be in sight as soon as men recognize the significance of black sheep. When that day dawns, all the controversialists will begin to pay some respect to the exception. It is useless to ignore it, to brush it aside with the suave assertion that '*the exception proves the rule.*' Unless you are very careful, the exception may be the death of you. There is a story told—I think it appeared in the *Spectator*—of an Englishman who visited Ireland in the days of the Land League, and was assured by an optimistic Irish landlord that there was no crime and no violence in that distressful country. All the assertions to the contrary, he said, were malicious inventions. The Englishman had scarcely passed out of the lodge-gates when a bullet passed through his hat. Returning to the house, he demanded to know the meaning of the outrage.

'I thought,' he exclaimed, 'that you said that there was no crime in Ireland. Look at this!' and he pointed to the hole through his hat.

'Oh,' replied the optimist, calmly, 'that's nothing! It's just a blackguard in the shrubbery!'

Merely an exception, you observe! But did the exception prove the rule?

It is the exception that matters. Mr. Ian Macpherson, M.P., was impressing this on a company of London journalists the other evening. And, to illustrate his point, he told of an editor who said to a young reporter, 'Now, suppose you walk along the Strand and see a dog biting a man, *that* is not news. But, on the other hand, suppose you walk along the Strand and see a man biting a dog, *that* is first-class news!' We must keep our eye on the blackguard in the shrubbery! We must look out for the man that bites the dogs! We must pay marked attention to the black sheep! When all the optimists face frankly the disquieting factors in the situation; when all the pessimists take note of the bright light that is in the cloud; when all the politicians consider seriously and applaud honestly the strong planks of their opponent's platforms; and when all men have eyes to discern the virtues of those from whom they differ; then, as I say, the millennium cannot be long delayed. As it is, we persuade ourselves that we are right and the other fellow wrong. And when, in an awkward moment, it is demonstrated that, on one point at least, the other fellow is right, and we ourselves wrong, we wave our hands with a fine assumption of superiority and fall back upon the stock contention. 'Oh,' we say, 'that is the exception, and the exception, you know, proves the rule!' But, unhappily for us, the exception does nothing of the kind.

Darwin held that the exception is the end of the rule; it strikes the rule its death-blow. Once the exception appears, the rule no longer exists. Through long years of patient investigation he would discover that thousands of specimens, in given circumstances, would behave in a particular way. The evidence would appear overwhelming; but, just as he was about to generalize on these harmonious observations, and announce his conclusion, he would suddenly come upon a specimen that, under identically similar conditions, behaved in a different way. It would have been the easiest thing in the world to have dismissed the awkward phenomenon with the cheap sophistry that the exception proves the rule. But so plausible a way of escape is inconsistent with the best traditions of scientific research, and the premature conclusion was immediately abandoned as untenable. 'The little beast is doing just what I did not want him to do!' Darwin would exclaim; and, out of respect for the newly discovered exception, he reserved his judgement on the mass of evidence previously collected. It was this reverence for the exception that led him to wait twenty-nine years before publishing his conclusions on the habits of earthworms, and that impelled him to spend fifteen years in revising the manuscript of his epoch-making book. He recognized with absolute candour that the exception is at least as much a revealer of scientific truth as the rule, and that everything is to be lost by surrendering to the dishonesty that would ignore it.

The thing that makes humanity so perennially fascinating is its infinite capacity for exceptions. Compare men with money, for example. I go to a bank and draw a thousand sovereigns. I carry them home and shoot them out in a glittering pile upon the table. I run my fingers through them. Each sovereign in the shining hoard is worth precisely two hundred and forty pence. There is not one that would bring me two hundred and forty-one pence; there is not one that is worth only two hundred and thirty-nine. But take a thousand men or, better still, take a thousand boys! As Browning says:

> You see lads walk the street
> Sixty the minute; what's to note in that?
> You see one lad astride the chimney-stack,
> Him you must watch.

Here is the exception; and it is the exception, the poet says, that you must watch—the exception astride the chimney-stack! Thousands of boys passed Bothwell Castle. Scores of them never glanced up at the stately old ruin, nor asked a question as to its romantic story. But one boy climbed to the very top and, whilst onlookers held their breaths, carved his name where no boy had ever carved his name before. I doubt if anybody has ever clambered to that dizzy height for the sake of reading that stony autograph. But, if any one did, he was rewarded for his scramble by beholding the name of DAVID LIVINGSTONE. *He* is the 'lad astride the chimney-stack.' *He* is the exception. '*Him* you must watch!' New continents slumber in his brain. And, speaking of Livingstone, I am reminded of something else. It may be that, when Jesus spoke of the '*other sheep*' that He had, the sheep which were '*not of this fold*,' He was thinking of *black* sheep! Livingstone certainly thought so; and the fact that the text about the '*other sheep*' adorns his tomb at Westminster Abbey emphasizes the idea.

The finest thing ever said in praise of black sheep was said by Carlyle. He is speaking of the exception. 'The world's wealth,' he avers, 'is in its original men. By these and their works it is a world and not a waste. Their memory and their record are its sacred property forever.' And, in his essay on "Circles," Emerson says that the arrival upon the planet of an original thinker is like the outbreak of a fire in a great city—nobody knows where it will end! Clearly, therefore, the exception is entitled, not only to consideration, but to supreme consideration. It is the one arresting and outstanding feature on the horizon.

Macaulay declares that, in this matter, Protestantism has a great deal to learn from Catholicism. If, he says, an enthusiast of daring ideas and flaming passion appears in the Anglican Church he is frowned down and becomes the Church's most dangerous enemy. But if such a figure arises in the Church of Rome, she makes a champion of him. She makes him the head of a new order, covers him with a gown and hood, ties a rope round his waist and sends him forth to teach in her name. As a result, he becomes as strongly attached to the

Church as are any of the cardinals whose scarlet carriages and liveries crowd the entrance of the palace on the Quirinal.

'Thus,' says Macaulay, 'place Ignatius Loyola at Oxford. He is certain to become the head of a formidable secession. Place John Wesley at Rome. He is certain to be the first general of a new society devoted to the interests and honour of the Church. At Rome the Countess of Huntingdon would have a place in the calendar as St. Selina; and Mrs. Fry would be foundress and first Superior of the Blessed Order of Sisters of the Gaols. It is,' Macaulay declares, 'impossible to deny that the polity of the Church of Rome is the very masterpiece of human wisdom; in truth, nothing but such a polity could, against such assaults, have borne up such doctrines.' The Roman Church, that is to say, owes, not only her enormous prestige, but her very existence, to her recognition of the value of black sheep.

Why, one of the loveliest tales ever told is a story of the exception. How does it run?

> There were ninety and nine that safely lay
> In the shelter of the fold;
> But one was out on the hills away,
> Far off from the gates of gold.
> Away on the mountains wild and bare,
> Away from the tender Shepherd's care.

It is not a mere matter of arithmetic—ninety-nine here and one out yonder. There is more in it than that. The question arises: Why did the one wander whilst the ninety and nine stayed at home? It was because there was originality, individuality, imagination, curiosity, and enterprise in that one. It was abnormal, extraordinary, exceptional. And the parable, if it means anything, means that the odd sheep is worth saving.

The parable that immediately follows it—the parable of the Prodigal Son—bears precisely the same significance. The prodigal was the black sheep of the family. Yet we all love him better than the white sheep that never wandered. Henry Drummond says that some men are kept by sheer cowardice from going astray. 'They have not character enough to lose their character. For it often requires a strong character to go wrong. It demands a certain originality and courage before a man can make up his mind to fall out of step with society and scatter his reputation to the winds. So it comes to pass that many very mean men retain their outward virtue; and conversely, among the prodigal sons of the world are found characters of singular beauty.'

I do not mean that the best men go astray. And most certainly I do not mean that any man is the better for having gone astray. I mean that the waywardness of the prodigal is merely the expression of his exceptional quality; and that, if that exceptional quality had been earlier recognized and skilfully developed, it might have found some happier expression than his migration to the far country. Black sheep are, in the beginning, black lambs. And black lambs need careful shepherding. Those into whose flocks black lambs come will be wise to learn by heart one of the earlier sentences of this essay. Morning, noon, and night, let them say to themselves, 'black lambs are not *bad* lambs; they are merely *exceptional* lambs; and between the *exceptional* and the *vicious* there is all the difference in the world.'

Charles Wagner says a few wise words about black lambs, although he does not call them by that name. 'Let the family distinguish these singular children,' he says. 'Just because they are unlike anybody else, they have more need that we should love and cherish them. We must interpret their oddities with indulgence and sympathy. Take care! The awkwardness, shyness, and timidity, the disconcerting fashions that some little fellow has, are perhaps the formless cocoon whence one day shall burst forth an incomparable butterfly.'

'How can I ever forget,' Dr. Talmage used to say, 'the visit to the home of my boyhood of Truman Osborne, the evangelist? He had a wonderful skill in winning people. One evening we were seated round the fire. He turned to my father and said, "Mr. Talmage, are all your children Christians?" "Yes," answered my father, "all but De Witt."'

'*All but De Witt!*'—here is the black sheep, the exception, the odd one! But I have interrupted the doctor's story!

'Then,' he goes on, 'Mr. Osborne looked down into the fireplace and began to tell a wonderful tale of a terrible storm that swept over the mountains, and all the sheep were in the fold; *all but one.*'

'*All but one!*'—here is the exception, the odd one! But again I have interrupted the narrative!

'Mr. Osborne told us that one sheep was away on the hills, perishing in the storm. Had he looked me in the eye as he told of that wayward sheep,' Dr. Talmage goes on, 'I should have been angered at the telling of the story; but he looked straight into the fire, and it was so pathetically and beautifully done that I never found any peace until I was sure I was inside the fold where the other sheep are!'

Black sheep are worth shepherding. There is joy in the presence of the angels over one sinner that repenteth more than over ninety and nine just persons that need no repentance. It is the exception that matters. All heaven welcomes the odd one.

IV

TAMMAS

I

It was just getting dusk. Unwilling to go in, I was lingering in the garden till the last moment, pulling up a weed here and cutting out a rose-sucker there. Then, just as I was bidding goodnight to God's great out-of-doors, a gig rattled up to the gate. It was Dr. Driver of Deepwater Hill.

'Ah,' he exclaimed, glancing at the little heap of tufts and suckers at my feet, 'so you can't be content to live and let live; what harm have these poor things ever done you, I should like to know!' And then, changing his tone, he added, 'But seriously, I wondered if you had heard that poor old Tammas had a pretty bad turn the other night. I was sent for just before midnight, and I thought at first that there was very little hope for him. He appears to be making a good recovery, however, and I dare say he'll be all right for a while. But he mentioned your name several times in my hearing, so I thought I'd drop in and let you know.'

As I accompanied him back to his gig, I thanked him for the trouble he had taken, and promised to drive over to Deepwater first thing next morning.

'Good!' he replied, 'I know he'll be pleased to see you; and,' he added, laughing, 'you'll find him as full of figures as ever.'

Tammas was for many years the treasurer of the Mosgiel Church. He was the most tremendous statistician that I ever met. As I have elsewhere said, he invariably carried a notebook and a blue pencil; and whenever he opened the notebook we caught sight of pages and pages of figures. Tammas reduced everything to mathematics. He could tell us, not only the amount of the collection on any particular Sunday years ago, but the exact number of coppers, threepenny pieces, sixpences, shillings, and half-crowns of which it was composed. He averaged everything; tabulated everything; worked everything out to decimal points; and kept the most elaborate records. In his cupboards he preserved all the notebooks that he had ever carried; he had them dated and labelled; he could put his finger at a moment's notice on any particular blue pencil computation that he had ever made.

It was a fearsome thing to contradict Tammas. At our deacons' meetings his statements were never questioned. If his brother-officers agreed with him, they said so. If not, they let it pass in silence. For they knew that, on the slightest provocation,

Tammas would deluge them with a cataract of comparative statistics.

After the doctor's departure, I walked round and told Gavin, our secretary, of the disquieting news that had reached me. Gavin thought all the world of Tammas, although no one had a greater dread of those formidable notebooks than had he.

'I'd like to go with you,' Gavin exclaimed, 'and, if you'll let me, I'll drive you over. Jeanie has been eating her head off in the stable for the last fortnight, and it will do her good to have a run. What time would you like me to call at the manse?'

We soon arranged details. At ten o'clock next morning we were climbing the road that winds up the slopes of Deepwater Hill, and, before noon, we were driving up the long avenue of tall blue-gums that leads up to Tammas's homestead.

II

Propped up by pillows, he was lying on a couch that had been placed beside the window. His face, rugged as granite, yet not without an indefinable expression of kindliness, showed indubitable signs of the ordeal through which he had passed. He grasped our hands in silence; there was a moisture in his eyes; he evidently felt like a man who had been passing through deep waters and was glad to find his feet once more on firm ground. His ruling passion was still strong upon him, however, for a notebook lay upon the rug that was wrapped about him, the blue pencil adorned the window-sill within reach of his hand, and his well-worn Bible reposed upon his pillow.

'Yes,' he said at last, 'it was touch-and-go with me. I've been nearer to the gates of heaven than I've ever been before; and it makes a man think, I can tell you. The doctor's patched me up a bit, but I don't suppose it's for very long; and, since I've been able to get to the couch here, I've been reading all that the Bible says about heaven. And I'm bound to say that it fairly astonished me. Why, in one place it even goes into figures, and I've been working them out this morning in my notebook. Somehow, I had never noticed before that the Bible gives the dimensions of the heavenly city. Man, it's wonderful! It took my breath away. Did you ever preach about it?'

He handed me his Bible and pointed to the sixteenth verse of the twenty-first chapter of the Book of Revelation. The margin contained a big cross, made by his unerring and terrible pencil. I read aloud:

'And the city lieth four-square, and the length is as large as the breadth, and he measured the city with the reed, twelve thousand furlongs. The length and the breadth and the height of it are equal.'

I had to confess that I had never preached on that glowing theme. In the exercise-book in which I entered suggestions for possible sermons, I had scrawled across the top of one page the words, *The City Foursquare*—but that was as far as it went. I had a hazy idea of emphasizing the point that the city is perfectly symmetrical.

Our conceptions of heaven are sometimes so sentimental, and at other times so stern, that the city of our fancy is rather forbidding than enticing. But the fault is in ourselves. In his *First Men in the Moon*, Mr. H. G. Wells makes his hero attempt to describe the earth and its inhabitants to the Grand Lunar. But the attempt is a ludicrous failure. The description was incomprehensible, for the visitor from the earth found that 'it is impossible to describe the phenomena of one world in the phraseology of another.' I suppose that is why the pictures of heaven that have been painted for us have seemed so grotesque and unconvincing and unattractive. 'I will one day preach a sermon,' I had said to myself, when I made that crude entry in my exercise-book, 'I will one day preach a sermon in which I will show that there is nothing extravagant or distorted about the reality. The city is shapely and splendid and symmetrical—a City Foursquare.' But it was only a crude suggestion, an amiable intention; the sermon had never been preached.

'No, Tammas,' I said, 'I've never taken that text. But I want you to tell me what I'm to say about it when I do. What have you been figuring out with your blue pencil? A minister is entitled to consult a commentary, you know; and I should like to know what you've been writing in your notebook.'

He smiled—a wan but gratified smile—and reached out his hand for the notebook on the rug.

III

'Did you ever think about the size of the city?' he asked. And, without waiting for a reply, he proceeded to reveal the significance of his statistics. 'Man, it's amazing; it's astounding; it beats everything I ever heard of! John says that each of the walls of the city measures twelve thousand furlongs. Now, if you work that out'—he bent closely over his notebook—'it will give you an area of 2,250,000 square miles! Did you ever hear the like of that? The only "city foursquare" that I ever saw was Adelaide in South Australia. The ship that brought me out from the Old Country called in there for a couple of days, and I thought it a fine city. But, as you know very well, the city of Adelaide covers only one square mile. Each of the four sides is a mile long. London covers an area of one hundred and forty square miles. But this city—the City Foursquare! It is 2,250,000 times as big as

Adelaide! It is 15,000 times as big as London! It is twenty times as big as all New Zealand! It is ten times as big as Germany and ten times as big as France! It is forty times as big as all England! It is ever so much bigger than India! Why, it's an enormous continent in itself. I had no idea of it until I went into the figures with my blue pencil here.'

He would allow no comment at this stage. 'Wait a minute,' he pleaded, as Gavin turned to ask a question, 'wait a minute—I've been going into the matter of population, and it's even more wonderful still. Look at this! Working it out on the basis of the number of people to the square mile in the city of London, the population of the City Foursquare comes out at a hundred thousand millions—seventy times the present population of the globe!'

I confessed that the figures were both startling and suggestive; but Gavin, who was always on the look-out for some weak point in his old friend's armour, made an opportunity to ask the question that, at an earlier stage, Tammas had forbidden.

'Ay, but Tammas,' remonstrated Gavin, 'aren't you taking it just rather literally? It's a spiritual revelation, ye ken, and it seems to me that it's to be understood metaphorically, as you may say; I never heard of working out the Book of Revelation by arithmetic before.' But Tammas had anticipated the objection and was ready for him.

'To be sure! To be sure!' he replied, 'I was coming to that, Gavin, if you'd let me go on. For that's just the beauty of the whole thing. As you say, the words are not to be taken literally. They're what ye may call symbolical. But, then, Gavin, you never heard of a symbol that was bigger than the thing that it symbolized. When I was a laddie and went to school away in the Old Country, the teacher used to hold up an orange. "The earth," she would say, "is like this orange!" Of course I never went to measure the orange to see how big the earth was. I understood that the thing that the orange symbolized was millions of times as big as the orange itself. And if you tell me that this City Foursquare is symbolic, you only make the reality millions of times bigger than I have shown. As the orange is to the earth, so are these statistics'—he glanced at his notebook—'to the City of the Lord. Do you see?' Gavin was apparently satisfied, for he raised no further objection.

I thought I saw symptoms of fatigue in the old man, so I rose.

'Well, Tammas,' I said, in taking leave of him, 'now that I know what your blue-pencil commentary contains, I shall certainly preach one fine day soon on *The City Foursquare*.'

'It will have to be a missionary sermon,' he answered, 'for where are all the people to come from to fill the city with life? It will take all China and Africa and India and all the other continents and islands to provide the millions of millions that that city will hold. And,' he added, as he took my hand, 'you'll see, when you look the passage up at home, that it's meant to be a missionary vision. It talks about the gates—the twelve gates—three to the East, three to the West, three to the North, and three to the South. I wondered, when I read it, if that was what Jesus had in mind when He said that *they shall come from the East and the West and from the North and from the South and sit down in the kingdom of God.*

'But, however that may be, you'll find when you study it that you can't preach any sermon but a missionary sermon on the City Foursquare. The vision of the City Foursquare is a missionary vision, and the twelve gates are the secret of its deeper meaning. You will see what I mean when you prepare your sermon; I hope I may be back in my old place to hear it.'

Five minutes later, Gavin and I were driving up the long avenue to the Mosgiel Road, and Jeanie, with her head to her stable, was evidently determined to leave Deepwater behind her as quickly as possible.

IV

In the solitude of my study I soon discovered that Tammas was right. The vision that Jesus gave to John on the isle that is called Patmos was, above everything else, a great missionary vision. The seer forgot the tiny rock, riddled with its mines, on which he lay, and saw this splendid city which he was to help in building—the City Foursquare. Its magnitude—the magnitude revealed in Tammas's notebook—rebukes our intellectual narrowness and theological littleness and denominational exclusiveness! It is glowing, grand, glorious! One's blood tingles at the very thought of it! Neither in prose nor in poem is there anything that can compare with it!

I found that Tammas was right, too, in saying that *the twelve gates* are the key to the meaning of the vision. As I glance at the map I see that, in a peculiar way, the world divides itself up from Patmos as the apple does from the core. To the *north* are the great modern empires; to the *south* the vigorous young colonial dependencies; to the *east* the peoples whose stories are hoary with antiquity; to the *west*, the alert, aggressive Occidental nations.

Three gates to the *East!* The eastern gates look out upon Persia, Arabia, and the Orient. What memories of magicians and astrologers; of Ali Baba; of Sinbad the Sailor; what hoards of graceful romance and quaint old Eastern legend rush to mind as we think of those dreamy Eastern peoples! As they were in the beginning, so they are and ever shall be. The East is a panorama of colour; of strange, flowing costumes; of ancient and changeless customs. The East is drowsy, conservative, antiquated. And the City Foursquare flings open three of its gates to that sleepy old world. Let all our missionaries in India, in China, and among the ancient Oriental peoples, take fresh heart!

Three gates to the *West!* There is room in the City Foursquare for everything that is up-to-date, everything that is wide-awake, everything that is restless and impatient of stagnation. The City Foursquare throws open three of its great gates to the people of the later civilizations—the people of the motor-car, the aeroplane, and the wireless telegram. It is like a tonic to think of those two worlds—the patient Orient and the pushful Occident—meeting and mingling as they press through eastern and western gates into the City Foursquare!

Three gates to the *North!* The City Foursquare offers its spacious hospitalities to the people of the Motherland and of the mighty nations round about her!

Three gates to the *South!* We who spend our lives beneath the Southern Cross like to think of that.

There is a place for us—the younger peoples, the nations of tomorrow—in the City Foursquare!

V

I preached that missionary sermon to my Mosgiel people, but Tammas did not live to hear it. A month or two after the incidents that I have here recorded, he slipped quietly away. His mind wandered slightly at the last. 'My *pencil!*' he said; and, to humour him, they placed it in his hand. 'My *notebook!*' and they laid it on the pillow near his head. 'My *reed!*' he demanded; and they were puzzled. It was only afterwards that they remembered: '*he measured the city with the reed, twelve thousand furlongs.*'

Gavin did not long survive him. A few months after the preaching of that missionary sermon, without a second's warning or a sign of feebleness, he suddenly left us. And today, sitting here at my desk, I like to think that those rugged but valiant comrades of my earliest ministry are reunited, and reunited amidst the sanctities and splendours of *the City Foursquare*.

V

THE BATTERY

The Arnolds were giving a Christmas party. There had been blind-man's-buff, hunt the slipper, family coach, musical chairs, and all the other time-honoured games. There had been, too, a Christmas tree; each hand held some magic gift that had mysteriously grown upon the branches that were gaily lit with fairy-lamps; and each flushed face was surmounted by the frail and fantastic millinery that had issued from the interior of the bon-bons. Mrs. Arnold had suddenly vanished; it was whispered that she had gone to prepare the snapdragons; and, during the momentary lull in the evening's frolic, Mr. Arnold announced that he had something locked up in his office along the passage; but he warned his guests that it would bite! It turned out to be an electric battery. Jean Gillespie offered to take the first shock. She was soon writhing and screaming.

'Let go!' cried Ruth, her sister, sympathetically.

'I can't!' replied poor Jean. And in that *'I can't!'* she stated, as forcefully as it is possible to state it, one of the cardinal laws of life. It represents one of the first principles of human existence. There are few difficulties greater than the difficulty of letting things go.

The contents of the universe may be divided into two classes. When God made His world, He made it a world of Men and of Things. Either would have been incomplete without the other. If He had made it a world of Things without Men, it would have been without form and void, and darkness would have been upon the face of the deep, and the Spirit of God could never have moved upon the face of the waters. If He had made it a world of Men without Things, those men would have been the picture of utter helplessness. It is by means of Things that Men achieve their triumphs; it is by becoming the agents and instruments of Men that Things come to their own.

Although they seem to possess nothing in common, these two—Men and Things—are incessantly entering into partnership the one with the other. These partnerships, once made, are almost indissoluble. The two grow to each other. A man picks up a Thing, and it is of very little use to him until it becomes an integral part of his being. In his *Gamekeeper at Home*, Richard Jefferies describes the gamekeeper's gun. The varnish is worn from the stock by incessant friction against his coat. It has been his companion for so many years that it is not strange he should feel an affection for it; no other ever fitted the shoulder so well or came with such delicate precision to its position. 'So accustomed is he to its balance and hang in the hand that he never thinks of aiming; he simply looks at the object, still or moving, throws the gun from the hollow of his arm, and instantly pulls the trigger, staying not a second to glance along the barrel. It has become almost a portion of his body, answering like a limb to the volition of his will.' It would be easy to multiply such examples. We could summon, if we needed their evidence, the woodman and his axe, the batsman and his bat, or the warrior and his sword. In each case the Man and the Thing become one.

Especially the warrior and his sword. For Jean Gillespie, unable to let go, reminds me of Eleazar the son of Dodo the Ahohite. Of all David's mighty men, Eleazar was reckoned among the foremost three. His distinguishing exploit occurred on a day when the fighting men were absent from the camp. Eleazar was left on guard; and, to his astonishment, the enemy suddenly appeared. '*And Eleazar arose and smote the Philistines, until his hand was weary.*' And, even then, he declined to surrender. '*And his hand clave unto his sword, and the Lord wrought a great victory that day.*' The best exposition of the incident occurs in *Chicot the Jester*. 'You see, Remy,' Dumas makes one of his characters to say, 'when my arm holds a sword, it becomes so identified with it that the fibres of the flesh take the hardness and the spring of the steel, and the steel seems to become animated and warm like living flesh. From that moment my sword is an arm, and my arm a sword. So that, do you see, there is no longer any question of strength or energy. A sword does not become fatigued.' That was Eleazar's experience exactly. 'Eleazar fought the enemy single-handed,' says Mr. S. D. Gordon. 'Up and down, left and right, hip and thigh, he smote with such terrific earnestness and drive that the enemy broke and fled. And the muscles of his hand became so rigid around the handle of his sword that he could not tell by the feeling where his hand stopped and his sword began. Man and sword were one.'

John Bunyan must have been thinking of Eleazar when he painted on his broad canvas the picture of Mr. Valiant-for-Truth. Toward the end of their pilgrimage, Christiana and her company came to the place where Mr. Little-Faith was robbed, and they found there a man with his sword drawn and his face all smeared with blood. His name, as it turned out, was Mr. Valiant-for-Truth, and he had been attacked by three desperate ruffians, against whom he fought gallantly.

'You fought for a great while,' remarked Mr. Greatheart. 'I wonder you were not weary.'

'I was,' replied the wounded man; 'I fought till my sword did cleave to my hand; and when they were joined together, as if the sword grew out of my arm, then I fought with most courage!'

'I can't let go!' cries Jean.

'His hand clave unto his sword,' says the inspired record, in reference to Eleazar.

'It was as if my sword grew out of my arm,' exclaims Mr. Valiant-for-Truth.

'The gamekeeper's gun is almost a portion of his body,' says Richard Jefferies. 'It answers like a limb to the volition of his will.'

So do Things grow to Men and Men to Things. The law affects us all and affects us all the time. Day and night it is in ceaseless operation. Indeed, it is at night that we are most forcibly reminded of its power. For at night, like Jean, we find it most difficult to relax our hold upon things. The art of falling asleep is the art of leaving go. But it is not easy. We most of us have our hands full all day. And we discover, when bedtime comes, that it is difficult to empty them. We have clung to those things so long, and have grasped them so tenaciously, that our rigid muscles cleave to them in the darkness. I went the other day to see a great cricket match. The conditions were ideal; the day was perfect; the game was crowded with incident and excitement; and I enjoyed it to the full. Then, after a restful evening on the lawn, spent in discussing the thrills of the day, I went to bed. But not to sleep. As soon as my eyes were closed I saw once more that sensational catch in the slips; again I watched the ball as it went soaring over the pavilion; and a second time I saw England's greatest batsman beaten by a ball that sent his middle stump somersaulting across the ground. I turned this way and that way in the darkness and tried to forget; but, like Jean, I could not let go. A man may retire for the night; by closing his bedroom door he may shut the whole world out; by closing his eyelids he may shut his soul securely in; yet, unless he has managed matters with rare shrewdness and discretion, he will still find his hand cleaving to his ledgers, his cheque-book, and his correspondence. A woman may turn her back upon the universe; and, worn with a multitude of cares, may abandon herself to the rest that she has so thoroughly earned; yet, unless she has mastered the high art of leaving go of things, she will find her hand still cleaving to the helm of the home.

'Let go!' cried Ruth Gillespie. 'I can't!' screamed Jean. Very few of us can.

It is a curious and interesting study in psychology to watch the mind, during the early days of a holiday, relaxing its hold upon things. During the first part of our stay at the seaside, we enter dreamily into its delights. We can scarcely realize that we are where we are. As soon as the mind is set free from some actual occupation, it flies back, like a twig that has been first bent and then released, to the environment to which it is accustomed. The body is resting on the sands, but the soul is back at the warehouse or the shop. Gradually, however, the old life fades away. The mind grows at home on the beach. The waves become focal; the warehouse becomes marginal. It is with a start, like the start with which we are awakened from a sound sleep, that we are reminded of the world that we have forsaken. We have relaxed our hold at last.

It is good—as Jean Gillespie must have felt that night—to be able to let go. We often destroy our difficulties, as the kookaburra destroys the snakes, by dropping them. When a problem proves particularly baffling, it is best to let go. Sleep over it. The muscles of the mind, wearied with the tussle, relax their feverish grip; and, when they take the matter up again, their grasp is fresh and vigorous and keen. I suppose that every man who writes much arrives, every now and again, at a point beyond which he cannot clearly see his way. How should the thought be arranged? How should the argument be developed? Shall I proceed in this way or in that way? He lays down his pen, leans back in his chair, and weighs the advantages of each method. But, in doing so, a fresh suggestion occurs to him, and thus the problem becomes more involved than ever. If he takes my advice, he will sit worrying about it no longer. Let him leave it. Let him go and dig a root of potatoes, or drink a glass of milk, or wash his hands—or all three—and, nine times out of ten, by the time that he gets back to his desk his course will be as clear as the king's highway.

Nine times out of ten. But what of the tenth time? What if, having drunk the milk and dug the potatoes and washed his hands, he finds, on returning to the desk, that the way is still obscure? He must still do as the birds do. The jackasses drop the small snakes a little way; but they lift the big ones to a good height before dropping them. Our bewildered scribbler must take the hint. He has dropped his difficulty a little way, but its back is not broken. Let him try again. Put the manuscript aside for the day; turn to another theme; or, better still, close the desk, draw the blind, shut up the room, and go out.

I myself have had a curious experience in this connexion. I formed the habit, whenever my pen found itself in difficulties, of laying it aside and going for a walk. We all have our favourite walks, and my feet involuntarily turned, on these occasions, in the one direction. I promised myself that I would forget, as quickly as possible, all about the unfinished manuscript upon the desk. On returning from my excursion, I was generally astonished at the thoroughness with which I had kept my promise. For the first quarter of a mile, the problem that had perplexed me as I sat at the desk would rush at me again and again, and call me a coward for turning my back upon it. But, on reviewing the outing, I could generally recall the exact spot at which the troublesome question presented itself for the last time. It was under the big elm-tree at the corner, or at the white seat under the pines, or in crossing the bridge from which I watched the water-rat, that my mind let go. And when, later on, I entered my study, drew up the blind, and resumed my place at the desk, I was invariably astonished at the simplicity of my task.

We have a stupid way of supposing that we are masters of the things that we hold. Jean Gillespie knew better. We are often the slaves of the things that we hold; we are masters of the things that we can drop. Horace Mansfield used to tell of a tragedy that he witnessed at Niagara. A dead sheep was floating towards the falls. Suddenly a vulture wheeled about it, settled on the carcass, and greedily glutted its appetite on the feast of carrion. Mr. Mansfield took it for granted that, as the body neared the cataract, the bird would rise; but, to his amazement, it simply spread its wings and was carried with the sheep over the raging torrent. Mr. Mansfield put himself to some trouble to solve the mystery, and he succeeded. In the waters below the falls he found the carcass with the dead vulture still clinging to it. The bird had probably intended leaving its prey before the danger-zone was reached. But, on that bitter mid-winter's day, its talons had become frozen in the flesh of the sheep. Bird and beast were inextricably and inseparably attached to each other. The vulture was the victim of the thing that it held. It could not leave go.

What is this but a reflection, as in a mirror, of our great and baffling modern problems? The drunkard and the gambler are the slaves of the things that they hold. Nor are they alone. Many a man fancies himself the lord of the wealth that he holds; he does not recognize that his wealth has enslaved him. Or take another case. In his *Pictures and Problems from London Police Courts*, Mr. Thomas Holmes, who has probably had more practical experience of the criminal classes than any man of our time, has a good deal to say about this strange law. Nothing baffled him more than the persistency with which certain converted criminals relapsed into crime. He gives numerous instances; one example must serve our purpose.

The man, to whose story Mr. Holmes devotes several pages, was an excellent bookbinder—and an excellent burglar. The pity of it was that the bookbinder had become lost in the burglar. Mr. Holmes determined to reverse the process. Why should not the burglar vanish in the bookbinder? Magistrates, judges, and library people became interested; they gave the man work; and he soon won for himself a good position. He had home, money, friends—all that heart could wish. Clergymen, judges, and public men called on him and he on them. 'Exact, methodical, industrious beyond measure, honest in his dealings, he was to me a friend, a study, and a delight,' says Mr. Holmes.

But it was all to no purpose. He was caught breaking into a boot-warehouse! It was evidently not for the sake of the plunder. Five pounds of his own earnings were found on him when he was searched. 'I told him,' says Mr. Holmes, 'that I could not understand how such an intelligent, industrious, skilful workman as he was could be a burglar. He not only knew that it was wrong and a crime, but he also knew that it was folly and could not pay. He looked at me for a moment, and then said: "You have seen the power of drink and you know the fascination of gambling. Bring drink, gambling, horse-racing, and roll them into one, and they do not equal the fascination of burglary. The silence of the night, every sense on the alert, the element of danger, the chances of success and failure, all combine to make burglary a fascination. Why do some men get drunk? Because they must. So I was a burglar because I was compelled to be a burglar."

'There was no doubt about the truth of this,' adds Mr. Holmes, 'it admitted of no argument, for his manner of saying it was quite convincing.' It was another illustration of the difficulty of relaxing one's grip. Like Jean Gillespie, he could not let go; he was the victim of the thing that he held.

But, before closing, we must lift the matter to a loftier plane. I am the son of a college that has for its crest a cross grasped by a hand. The motto beneath it reads: *Et teneo et teneor—I hold and am held.* The only things worth holding are the things that we cannot let go. '*I will speak no more in His name,*' exclaimed Jeremiah, but he discovered that it was more difficult than he supposed to withdraw from his prophetic office. '*I said, I will speak no more in His name; but His word was in mine heart as a burning fire shut up in my bones; I was weary with forbearing; I could not stay.*' His hand clave to his sword and he could not drop it at will. He reminds me of Polycarp, the angel of the church at Smyrna.

'Blaspheme Christ!' demanded the proconsul, when the aged minister was dragged into the arena.

'Eighty and six years,' he replied, 'have I served Him; how can I now blaspheme my King and Saviour?'

His hand clave unto the cross; he could not loose his hold; he held it and it held him.

Even God Himself is subject to the same law. '*How shall I give thee up, O Ephraim?*' He asks. The sins of Ephraim have been multiplied and his follies cry aloud for judgement; yet the Hand that has held him for so long cannot easily relax its grasp. The pierced Hand that clasps mine becomes rigid in its hold. There is a Love that will not let me go.

VI

THE DARK-ROOM

The lure of the dark-room is indescribable. To a man who dabbles in photography, the dark-room is the witch's cavern and the magic grotto and the enchanted palace, all in one. To other eyes it may look dismal and bare. *He* knows better. He knows that the dark-room is alive with mystery and crowded with sensations. It is the haunt of a thousand thrills. It is the home of the most delicious surprises and of the most depressing disappointments. Smiles and sighs lurk in every crack and crevice of the gloomy place. He never knows what to expect next. A dark-room is one of the few places in which a man may become excited in silence and solitude. In the darkness the photographer forgets everything—even the darkness. The white plate is steeped in the fluid that is to woo from it the picture that it so mysteriously conceals, and the operator holds his breath. Two pictures occupy his fancy— the vivid and variegated picture that, captivating his eye, led him to set up his camera, and the photograph in black and white that he so soon hopes to possess. Will the picture on the plate be the picture of his dreams? The enthusiasm that surged through his soul when he pressed the bulb rushes back upon him in an intensified form. As the dim and shadowy figures appear upon the plate, he can almost hear the beating of his own heart, and his hand trembles slightly as it grasps the dish.

I am merely recording an experience that has recently befallen me. I have been to Beechington with my camera. During my stay there, I took quite a number of photographs. Most of them, I knew, would prove the veriest mediocrities—interesting only as domestic records. But one had stirred my very soul. It was a picture of the caves. Clambering over the reef, I saw them from a new angle, and was charmed with the opportunity that the scene presented. I determined to spare no pains in an endeavour to secure the picture that haunted my imagination. The gloomy recesses of the gigantic caverns; the massive boulders strewn about their yawning mouths; the great gaunt gums above; the breakers in the foreground and the towering peaks behind—all this made up an alluring combination of romantic features. If only I had the skill to do it justice! But it was difficult to judge the strength of the light and to gauge the exact exposure that the plate required. I took my time in focusing and arranging the camera. Nothing was likely to vanish and nothing was likely to intrude; there was every reason for acting leisurely. Watching the clouds, I selected with the greatest care the moment of exposure; and then, when all the conditions seemed ideal, I pressed the bulb. I am, however, only a novice, the veriest tyro. I am largely at the mercy of guess-work; and I could not, therefore, contemplate the result with any confidence. My uncertainty intensified my anxiety to get to the dark-room; and my eagerness to get to the dark-room added a fresh feverishness to my excitement when, in the dark-room, the critical moment came.

The critical moment is, of course, the moment at which the plate is removed from the developer. To my unbounded delight, I saw that my picture of the caves was a distinct success. More by good luck than by sound judgement, the exposure must have been perfect. As I bent over the developing-dish, I saw, first the bold outline, and then the microscopic detail, appear sharply and in vivid distinctness on the submerged plate. Every photographer knows the tense absorption of those anxious seconds.

Then comes the problem. When shall the negative be transferred to the fixing-bath? I am loath to remove it from the developer; another second or two may impart a finishing touch to the whole picture; the slightest impatience may rob the photograph of its chief charm. And yet, on the other hand, there comes a time at which the developing fluid begins to destroy its own work. The plate, left in this first dish, may be over-developed.

The picture becomes blurred through remaining in the bath too long. He is a very skilful photographer who knows the precise second at which to arrest the process of development by plunging the plate into the chemicals that will fix forever the impression it contains.

That crucial problem confronts us all. The soul and the sensitive plate are very much alike. Like the sensitive plate, the soul knows three really great moments—the moment at which it *receives* an impression, the moment at which it *develops* that impression, and the moment at which it *fixes* it. Quite automatically, the soul receives impressions from everything to which it is exposed. Some of the impressions received are not worth developing; and some of those developed are not worth fixing. But, every now and again, the soul enjoys an experience like my experience at the Beechington Caves. A particularly choice impression is received. But, unless it be most skilfully developed and most carefully fixed, the world at large will be none the better for it.

Have I ever told of 'the honeymoon couple' I met in Queensland? I was spending a very delightful holiday in that state. At the comfortable boarding-house which served as my head-quarters there were tourists from all over the world.

Some of them were extremely interesting— especially 'the honeymoon couple.' The pair who came to be called by that name consisted, not of a lady and gentleman, but of a girl and her camera. The two were inseparable. The girl was never once seen without her camera. She even brought it to table. She took photographs of everybody and everything. Every conversation was punctuated by the click of her shutter. And, when she was not arranging groups and snapping landscapes, she was talking of the groups that she had been arranging or of the landscapes she had recently snapped. Six weeks afterwards I met her in Melbourne. She was still carrying her camera. I politely inquired as to the success of her Queensland photographs. She burst into a peal of merry laughter.

'Oh,' she exclaimed, 'I never developed them. It would have been too much trouble. I enjoyed taking them. It was great fun to see people posing and trying to look pleasant. But when I was coming away, and found how many I had taken, I saw that I could never develop them. It would have taken ages. So I threw them all away'; and she broke into another peal of laughter.

It seemed very ridiculous when she told me, and I felt like scolding her. But, as I came home in the tram, it occurred to me that, over and over again, I had done the same kind of thing myself. While I stayed with the 'honeymoon couple' at that Queensland boarding-house. I must have exposed my soul to scores of impressions that I never took the trouble to develop. I saw things without pondering their intense significance; I heard things without realizing their importance and value; I read things without observing their bearing on my own life and its most pressing problems. I was introduced to people, shook hands, and let them go without recognizing that there was treasure in their minds and hearts by means of which *my* mind and *my* heart might have been permanently enriched. If only I had noted more carefully all that was shown me! If only I had memorized all that I heard! If only I had cultivated with some little care those new acquaintanceships! If only, at the end of each day, I had thrown myself into the armchair in my quiet room, closed my eyes, and mentally reviewed the adventures and experiences of the day! If only I had written then, and read afterwards, an account of some of the most pleasant and most profitable impressions that had come to me! But, alas, I did nothing of the kind. I spent the day taking photographs and was too lazy afterwards to develop them! I never expect to meet 'the honeymoon couple' again. The girl with the camera is arranging groups and snapping landscapes on other shores. I saw her name in the passenger list of the *Orvieto*. But I think more kindly of her than I did. For I have discovered that, however great her guilt may be, I myself am in the same condemnation.

Nature, strangely enough, goes to the other extreme. She is always developing her photographs, but never fixing them. You may tell her as often and as insistently as you will that, if the plate is left too long in the developer, it will become blurred. What does she care? 'Let them become over-developed!' she says, with a careless laugh. She has no fixing-bath. She brings her products to the point of ripeness, and then, instead of fixing them, lets them go on to rottenness. It is nothing to her. She has plenty more. It seems a thousand pities that this man, having come to his robust and vigorous prime, must now go on to his dotage; but Nature, having taken infinite pains in the process of development, refuses to fix. It seems a tragedy that this woman, having come to the full beauty and grace of her ripe maturity, must now go on to wrinkles, decrepitude, and decay. But Nature has no tears to shed over it; she does not care. The bloom on the peach may be exquisite. 'Let it rot!' she says. The petals of the rose may be perfect. 'Let them fall!' she exclaims. Nature is very much like the girl with the camera. The girl with the camera is always snapping but never developing. Nature is always developing but never fixing.

And, so far as I am under the authority of Nature, she sternly forbids my fixing things. When my last baby was born, I wished that she could remain a baby always. But Nature would not hear of it. In many a happy moment I have wished that I could crystallize my mood into an abiding experience.

> Oh, that I could forever stay
> In such a frame as this;
> I'd sit and sing myself away
> To everlasting bliss.

But Nature applies the 'move on' regulation. She hates stagnation.

Still, I cannot always take Nature as my model. Nature is a multi-millionaire. She can afford to bring her loveliest pictures to the point of perfect development, and then to spoil them by refusing to fix them. She knows that she herself will live forever and get plenty more. Why should she worry about *this* rose? She knows that she is the heiress of all the roses of a thousand unborn summers! Why should she trouble to perpetuate *this* peach? She knows that all the peaches of all the coming autumns will be hers! What, to her, is a handsome man or a lovely woman? Let them wither and shrivel and die! She has millions more to come—men still more stalwart and women still more charming. These are not worth the trouble of fixing. She likes to look at them as she develops them; and then she is content that they should perish. But I am not in a position to be so prodigal. I must feast my eyes on the beauty of every rose; I must make the most of the bloom on every peach. I must fix all my photographs. I must be warned by the example of the girl with the camera on the one hand and by the example of Nature on the other.

Nature herself recognizes this. She knows that I cannot do as she does. She, therefore, makes it easy for me to fix my photographs. There came to me the other day a helpful thought. It made me feel that life was well worth living. I pulled myself together and threw myself into my work with a heartier zest. Then, as I worked, a sudden fear took possession of me. 'Supposing,' I said to myself, 'supposing I forget the thought that made life seem so fair!' How could I fix the photograph that I had suddenly developed? And Nature, who never fixes her own photographs, taught me how I could fix mine. 'Repeat it!' she said. 'Pass the thought on to every man you meet! Weave it into every conversation and find a place for it in every letter. It will make life seem more rich and good to all whose lives touch yours; it will act upon them as a stimulus and a tonic; and, by constant repetition, the thought will become fixed and fastened among the treasures of your own memory!'

Every student of psychology knows that the man who, in the presence of some private calamity or public need, forms a noble and unselfish purpose, and then allows it to evaporate without crystallizing into action, is incalculably the poorer for the experience through which he has passed. His moral texture has been sensibly weakened. Under the spur of the emotion that swept over him, he should have told someone of his intention, or, in some other way, should have committed himself irretrievably to his splendid purpose. As it is, he has developed a photograph but has failed to fix it. It is worse than worthless: it is waste. It is not enough for me to gaze admiringly at the holy and beautiful resolve that is forming in my soul as, in the solitude of the dark-room, I gaze upon the lovely image in the dish. I must write it down, or tell somebody, or commit myself. The very act may beget a similar nobility in some other soul; it will at least fix the impression upon my own.

There are no back moves in the dark-room. If I fail to fix my photograph when it is at its best, I can never recapture the beauty I have squandered. My opportunity comes; it passes; it never comes again. I may afterwards look wistfully and regretfully at the ruined negative; I may reflect pensively on what might have been; but my steps can never be retraced.

Only last week I was talking to Andrew Duncannon. Andrew joined the church late in life, and nurses day and night a bitter regret. When he was scarcely more than a boy he heard Mr. Moody in London. 'I shall never forget that night,' Andrew was saying. 'Mr. Moody preached on *"Seek ye first the kingdom of God and His righteousness, and all these things shall be added unto you*." It seemed to me as if the gates of the kingdom of God stood wide open before me, and heaven and earth were both urging me to enter. I really meant at that moment to have done so. But somehow I allowed the occasion to slip by; I drifted out with the crowd; and it was nearly fifty years afterwards before I became a Christian. God is very pitiful,' he said, with evident emotion. 'God is very pitiful and of wondrous mercy; but life can never be what it might have been if I had done what I meant to have done that night!' Andrew was simply feeling, as I have so often felt, that the man who knows how to recognize life's critical moments when they come, and to fix his impressions on their arrival, is a very skilful photographer indeed.

VII

PARCEL-TIME

Even if I had no calendar—and no children—to remind me that Christmas was drawing near, I should still have no difficulty in hearing its footfall and discerning its approach. The violent epidemic of parcels that sweeps like a devouring pestilence over the entire community during the third week in December would startle me into a recognition of the fact that the festive season was once again knocking at my door.

The business of life requires me, once or twice a week, to travel by a particularly pleasant tramline. The road is flanked by graceful lawns, well-kept flowerbeds, noble avenues, and stately homes. The car is usually well filled; but during fifty-one weeks of the year I seldom see a parcel. On this tram-journey of mine, parcels are few and far between. It is considered unbecoming and undignified to carry them. But, when the first faint whispers of Christmas begin to be heard, all such delicacy is thrown to the winds. On my way home one fine December afternoon, I catch my first vision of brown paper and string. A lady will enter the tram carrying a parcel, and carrying it without shame. You feel as a man feels when he greets the first swallow of a new spring. You welcome it as a harbinger of the good time coming, and you know that you will soon see thousands more.

During the third week in December the graceful jacarandas that overhang the pathway beside the tramline, draping it with their gorgeous tassels of blue, and the brilliant hydrangeas that adorn the lawns with their splendour of delicate pink attain the climax of their glory. The law of association is capable of the oddest tricks and vagaries. There is no essential connexion between the bright petals and the drab parcels. Yet, as soon as I see the sheen of sapphire mantling the roadside, or the blaze of pink across the velvety lawns, I survey the ranks of my fellow-passengers to see if the first parcels of the season have yet made their appearance. The critic who tells me that, in associating beauteous petals with bulky parcels I am linking the essentially poetic with the essentially prosaic, has not yet discovered how much poetry may be wrapped up in a brown-paper parcel. I have! That is why I have taken up my pen today to write about parcels.

You have only to look at the lady who entered the tram with that first parcel of the season in order to be convinced that parcels are almost as poetic as petals. I have no idea what that package of hers contains; but she cannot conceal the secret satisfaction with which she is bearing it home. Moreover, that pioneer parcel is soon followed by scores of others. One swallow does not make a summer; and one parcel does not make a Christmas. But see how their numbers multiply! The day after that first lady entered the car with her parcel, half the people in the tram are carrying parcels! And, within a week, the person who makes himself conspicuous is not the man with a parcel, but the man with no parcels at all. As the tram passes one street after another, you see people bustling in all directions carrying parcels of all sorts, shapes, and sizes. Here, in the tram, are children with parcels, ladies with parcels, and even portly old gentlemen think it no surrender of their dignity to carry a parcel or two at Christmas-time. Some motherly bodies have transformed themselves into veritable parcels of parcels. They carry their parcels in groups and strings; parcels hang about them like bees in a swarm or grapes in a cluster. At every stopping-place the conductor helps a parcel-bedecked lady off the car, and assists another, laden like a merchantman's camel, to board the tram; and, although he shouts sternly, 'Hurry off, please!' and 'Hurry on, please!' you can, if you look closely, see a smile tucked away under his moustache. For he himself has boys and girls at home; and it may be that, at this very moment, his own wife, with a big parcel under each arm and a festoon of smaller ones hanging about her wrist and elbows, is being helped off some other tram by a comrade of the road.

That is the best of parcels. They have a social value. If I had gone to the platform at the rear of the tram and introduced each of those heavily-laden women to the conductor, the ceremony could not have broken down the barriers between them as effectively as the parcels did. For, after all, my formal introduction would have been a mere mentioning of names. 'Mrs. Smith—Conductor Jones'; 'Mrs. Robinson—Conductor Jones,' or something of that kind. It is all very correct—and very absurd. What in the world does the conductor learn concerning these two ladies as a result of my telling him their names? But the parcels! The parcels that he so politely hands to them are much more lavish in their distribution of essential information. If the knowledge of the ladies' names is of any value to him, the conductor can obtain it instantaneously by simply glancing at the labels. But, so profound is his contempt for the kind of information that my ceremonial introduction would afford him, that he scarcely glances at the labels: the parcels themselves have so much to say that is of far more absorbing interest. The foot of a china doll protruding from one parcel conveys to his mind the picture of a laughing girlish countenance that, bending over the face of a doll, takes to itself the pretty seriousness of fond motherly concern. The handle of a cricket-bat that has poked its way through the paper of another parcel summons to his fancy some roguish schoolboy features; whilst a parcel from the poulterer's makes him feel as if he had peeped into the home just as the family was sitting down to the great dinner of the year. How such an introduction puts to shame my poor repetition of colourless names! As he hands the parcels to and fro, they chatter to him at the rate of nineteen to the dozen, and tell him all about the homes that they are so soon to gladden.

It would be a more sociable and friendly world if people carried parcels all the year round. In the tram of which I have been speaking I used to see a tall gentleman whose personality attracted me. He had a strong, severe face: I felt that he must be a hard man, yet scrupulously just. He was sometimes accompanied by a lady, presumably his wife, to whom he was evidently deeply attached. I often felt that I should like to know more about them. One evening, just before Christmas, I saw him in the tram. Like the rest of us, he had a number of parcels. It occurred to me that I had not, for some months, seen the lady with him. And, as I examined him more narrowly, I fancied that he looked a little older and his face a trifle softer. These impressions still further inflamed my curiosity and deepened my desire to know him. But what could I do? He rose to leave the car at Wilmington Avenue: I was accustomed to ride as far as the terminus at Poynton Grove.

A sudden impulse seized me. It occurred to me that the walk home through Wilmington Avenue is only a few yards farther than the walk through Poynton Grove. As he was stepping from the car I rose hurriedly and followed him. For two or three hundred yards I walked a few feet behind him, wondering what had induced me to pursue so unusual a course. Then the unexpected happened. He dropped a small parcel. I picked it up, hurried after him, received his thanks and continued my walk by his side. We were introduced—and the parcel had done it. We have walked through Wilmington Avenue together many a time since. It was months before his marble reserve gave way to confidence, but he told me at last of the sorrows of his life—the sorrows that had culminated in the death of his wife—and I could see that my interest and sympathy had helped him.

Parcels are public property. I do not mean that I have a right to help myself to any small packages that happen to be insufficiently guarded. I mean that it is my duty to help myself to any information that they are eager to give and any opportunity that they are anxious to offer. As part of their social ministry, parcels give room for the play of life's small courtesies. One of the finest instances of this sort of thing occurs in the *Life of Sir Bartle Frere*. When Sir Bartle was returning to England after one of his diplomatic tours, it was the intention of Lady Frere to meet her husband at the train. At the last moment, however, she was prevented from doing so, and she had to instruct the coachman to go to the station alone.

'But, my lady,' the man protested, 'you forget that I have been engaged since Sir Bartle went abroad. How am I to recognize him?'

'Oh,' replied Lady Frere, 'that will be easy enough. Look out for a tall gentleman helping somebody!'

And, surely enough, the coachman found Sir Bartle assisting an old lady from the carriage with her parcels.

Now, when I speak of parcels, I am not thinking so much of their contents as of the paper and string. It is the paper and string that make the parcel a parcel. Take away the paper and string, and the parcel is no parcel at all. The doll wrapped up in paper and string is a parcel; the doll after the paper and string have been removed is a doll. That is why we always present the doll to the little girl with the paper and string still on it. In that way we give her two distinct and separate pleasures—the pleasure that arises from the *parcel-element* and the pleasure that arises from the *doll-element*. Every man, however matter-of-fact and prosaic, likes to receive his presents wrapped up in paper and string. He hesitates to cut the string; he prefers to untie the knot, to unfold the paper, and to come slowly upon the surprise awaiting him. The *contents-element* he will be able to enjoy for months or years; the *parcel-element* he can only enjoy for a few seconds or minutes; he therefore lingers over it that he may experience the pleasure to the full. It is a part—and a striking part—of our human love of mystery. It is a hint of the divinity that stirs within us.

I fancy that this homily of mine on parcels has been revolving in my brain longer than any other. It is the outcome of the first parcel with which I had to do—the first serious purchase that I ever made. My brother and I—he was five and I was seven—made up our minds when the autumn leaves were falling to buy a Christmas present for mother. How we saved our pennies! How we embraced any opportunity of earning an odd threepence! How feverishly we inspected every shop window in the town, searching for we knew not what. And at last, to our unbounded delight, we saw the very thing. There, in an ironmonger's window, we beheld a couple of stands on which it was intended that hot flat-irons should repose. We remembered having seen mother stand her irons on upturned plates and saucers. Oh, the wild excitement of that purchase; of handing over our hoarded savings; of receiving the parcel from the shopman; of smuggling it into the house after dark; of hiding it where mother would never come prematurely upon it! Oh, the terror with which we dreaded lest mother should buy herself a pair of iron-stands before Christmas came! And oh, the delirious ecstasy of at last producing the parcel, handing it to mother, watching her curiosity melt into surprised delight, and receiving her kisses of proud gratitude! What is it that Mr. Edgar Guest sings?

> In the Christmas time of the long ago,
> There was one event we used to know
>   That was better than any other;
> It wasn't the toys that we hoped to get,
> But the talks we had—and I hear them yet—
>   Of the gift we'd buy for Mother.
>
> If ever love fashioned a Christmas gift,
> Or saved its money and practised thrift,
>   'Twas done in those days, my brother—
> Those golden times of Long Gone By,
> Of our happiest years, when you and I
>   Talked over the gift for Mother.
>
> It had to be all that our purse could give,
> Something she'd treasure while she could live,
>   And better than any other.
> We gave it the best of our love and thought,
> And, oh, the joy when at last we'd bought
>   That marvellous gift for Mother!

I am not quite sure, but I fancy that those iron-stands are still to be seen in that dear old English home of mine. And, whenever I have caught sight of them, I have remembered that rapturous romance of early boyhood. It has helped me to understand—since our human emotions are only reflections of the divine—the joy that God must have found in presenting the world with the very gift that it needed.

There is one respect in which that first and greatest of all Christmas gifts resembles these parcels of ours. What is it that we sing at Christmas-time?

> Veiled in flesh the Godhead see,
> Hail the Incarnate Deity!

I have an old hymn-book in which the words are rendered:

> Wrapped in flesh the Godhead see,
> Hail the Incarnate Deity!

Wrapped in flesh! It is the phraseology of the parcel! The child's eyes sparkle as he catches a glimpse of the present through the paper. Human eyes have been entranced as they have beheld the unspeakable gift *'wrapped in flesh'*—the Deity Incarnate! They have never gazed upon its unveiled splendour. But they cherish in their hearts a wondrous secret. They know that the great manifestation is coming. They shall see Him as He is; they shall gaze with open face upon His glory ineffable; and even Christmas-time can bring to men no expectation more radiant than that.

Made in the USA
Middletown, DE
06 July 2017